Georgia Test Power

Grade 2

Printed in the U.S.A.

ISBN   978-0-544-21269-5

1 2 3 4 5 6 7 8 9 10   2266   22 21 20 19 18 17 16 15 14 13

4500428449   A B C D E F G

Contents

Introduction

What Is the *Georgia Test Power* Book?

The *Georgia Test Power* book is a workbook that helps you prepare to take the CRCT as well as transition to taking the PARCC tests of the Common Core State Standards. The questions in these tests are based on the skills you learn in school.

The Reading Practice Test in this book tests your reading and language arts skills. For some questions, you will read passages and answer questions about them. For other questions, you will read writing and answer questions about how to make the writing better. The Writing Practice Tests have you analyze and write in response to one or more texts. Reading/Writing Practice Tests have you read stories and articles and write answers to questions about them.

How to Use this Book

This book includes reading, language arts, and writing lessons. The reading lessons review skills that help you understand different kinds of reading material. The language arts and writing lessons review information important to helping you meet the Common Core State Standards.

You will get the most out of the reading experience if you ask yourself questions as you read:

- What is the passage mostly about?
- What do I already know about this topic?
- Is the passage making sense to me?
- Which parts do I need to reread?
- What can I do to understand words that I do not know?
- What did I learn from the passage?

You will get the most out of the language arts and writing experience if you do the following:

- Think about a plan before you write.
- Make a first try at the writing.
- Think about ways to make the writing better.
- Make changes to improve the writing.
- Think about citing sources and text details in your writing.

Learning to read and write well is like learning to ride a bike. The more you practice, the easier it becomes. Before you know it, you are riding with ease. So, let's hop on and get started!

Name _____ Date _____

Sequence of Events

How to Analyze the Text

In the story *Luke Goes to Bat*, the author tells what happens in the story in order. She tells what happens first, next, and last.

The things that happen in a story are called **events**. Most authors tell the events in a story in the order in which they happen. This order is called the **sequence of events**.

Special clue words called **time-order words** can help you understand the sequence of events. Time-order words include:

- *first, next, then, last, finally*
- *after, before, while*
- *today, yesterday, morning, afternoon, night*

Read this passage. Think about the order in which things happen. Then look at the chart that follows the passage.

> Tim cannot find his lunch for school. He looks on his desk. Then he looks on the kitchen table. Finally, he looks in his backpack. There is his lunch! It is right where he put it.

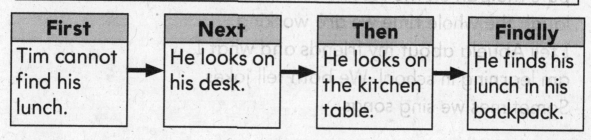

First	**Next**	**Then**	**Finally**
Tim cannot find his lunch.	He looks on his desk.	He looks on the kitchen table.	He finds his lunch in his backpack.

GO ON ▶

Apply to Text

Read the story. Then answer the questions.

Cooking with Abuela

1   My name is Tonya. Every Saturday, I go to Abuela's house. Abuela is my grandmother. She is teaching me how to cook.

2   My father drops me off early in the morning so I have all day to spend with Abuela. When I arrive, Abuela and I decide what we want to make. Together, we write a shopping list of everything we need. Then we go to the store.

Look Closely
Time-order words like morning help you know when events happen in a story.

3   At the store, Abuela shows me how to pick out fresh fruits, vegetables, and spices. She tells me, "Tonya, you always need to start with good food. If you start with good food then you will finish with good food."

4   Back at home, Abuela and I share the cooking jobs. First, I wash the fruits and vegetables. Next Abuela cuts up the food. Then I put the food in a pan. Abuela puts the pan on the stove. We talk and laugh the whole time we are working. I tell Abuela about my friends and what I am learning in school. We both tell jokes. Sometimes we sing songs.

5   We finish working in the afternoon. We play games while we wait for the food to cook. At just the right time, I get to taste everything. At last, we know that it is ready.

Look Closely

Time-order words like while help you know when events happen at the same time.

6   We set the table for dinner. In the evening, my mother and father come to eat with us. They enjoy dinner and say, "Tonya and Abuela are the best cooks we know!"

1 **What happens BEFORE Tonya and Abuela go to the store? Give TWO details from the story to support your answer.**

_____

_____

_____

_____

_____

GO ON ▶

2 What happens AFTER Tonya and Abuela finish working? Give TWO details from the story to support your answer.

_____

_____

_____

_____

_____

3 What is the LAST thing that happens in the story? Give details from the story to support your answer.

_____

_____

_____

_____

_____

STOP ⬡

Compare and Contrast

How to Analyze the Text

In the story "My Family," you learned how the people in Camilia's family are alike and different.

A Venn diagram is made up of two ovals. The part where the two ovals overlap in the middle shows how the things are alike. The outside parts of the ovals show how the things are different.

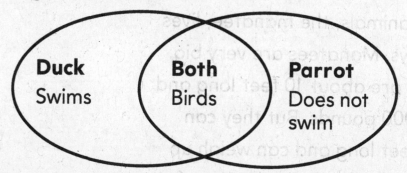

Duck
Swims

Both
Birds

Parrot
Does not swim

Read these sentences. Think about other ways in which ducks and parrots are alike and different.

Ducks and parrots are types of birds. They both have feathers, they both can fly, and they each lay eggs. One thing a duck can do that a parrot cannot do is swim. Ducks have webbed feet that look like flippers. The webbed feet help them swim in the water. Parrots do not have webbed feet. Still, they can do something a duck cannot do. Parrots can make human sounds. Some parrots even learn to say words!

Thinking about how things are alike and different can help you better understand what you are reading.

GO ON

Name _____ Date _____

Apply to Text

Read the passage. Then answer the questions.

Manatees and Dolphins

1   Manatees and dolphins are both mammals that live in the water. They are similar in some ways, and different in other ways.

2   One of these animals, the manatee, lives in rivers and bays. Manatees are very big. Most manatees are about 10 feet long and weigh about 1,000 pounds. But they can grow up to 14 feet long and can weigh up to 2,000 pounds. That's about the size of a small car!

3   Manatees are large, but they are not dangerous. They mostly eat plants that grow in the water. They swim very slowly, and they spend lots of time resting.

4   Sadly, manatees are not safe in water. Boats and ships sometimes run into manatees. Many manatees have died because of these collisions. People are working to help save the manatees from dying out.

5   Dolphins do not live in rivers. Instead, they live in bays and in the open ocean, where the water is salty. Dolphins need salt water to survive.

6   Dolphins are not as big as manatees. Most dolphins are about 7 feet long, though some can be a few feet longer. Dolphins also do not eat plants. Instead, they catch and eat fish and other small animals. They need to be fast swimmers to catch the animals they are chasing!

> **Look Closely**
>
> Parts of Paragraph 6 compare manatees and dolphins. How are they alike? How are they different?

7   Dolphins have some of the same problems as manatees. For instance, they can also be killed by boats. But there are many more dolphins than manatees. They are in no danger of dying out any time soon.

> **Look Closely**
>
> Are there lots of manatees in the water, or very few? Are there lots of dolphins in the water, or, or very few? How do you know?

1 **Which is true about manatees and dolphins?**

   A They are alike in some ways.

   B They are different in every way.

   C They are the same in every way.

   D They are animals that like each other.

1 (A) (B) (C) (D)

GO ON ▶

Name _____ Date _____

2 How are manatees and dolphins alike?

   A They both eat fish.

   B They are both able to walk on land.

   C They are both smaller than a butterfly.

   D They are both mammals.

Use the diagram below to answer Numbers 3 and 4.

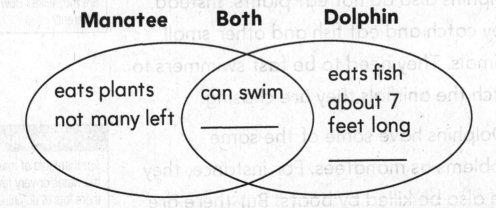

Manatee   Both   Dolphin

eats plants
not many left

can swim
_____

eats fish
about 7
feet long
_____

**3 Which of these goes on the blank line
under Both?**

   A swim very fast

   B do not eat plants

   C can live in bays

   D like to ride on boats and ships

> **Look Closely**
>
> The inside part of a Venn diagram tells how the two things are alike.

**4 Which of these goes on the blank line
under Dolphin?**

   A only 7 are left

   B larger than manatees

   C lives in rivers

   D needs salt water to live

2 Ⓐ Ⓑ Ⓒ Ⓓ

3 Ⓐ Ⓑ Ⓒ Ⓓ

4 Ⓐ Ⓑ Ⓒ Ⓓ   **STOP** ⬟

Name _____ Date _____

Language Arts

Skill Overview

A **sentence** is a group of words that has a subject and a verb and expresses a complete thought. Complete sentences make your writing clearer. Look at the chart to see how to fix sentences that are not complete.

Not Complete	Add a	Complete the sentence
Bought a boat.	subject	My dad bought a boat.
The class.	verb	The class lined up.

You use **punctuation** when you write sentences. Punctuation marks are symbols. Many punctuation marks come at the ends of sentences. Punctuation marks tell the reader how to read the sentence.

Statements and questions are types of sentences. A statement tells something. It ends with a **period**. A question asks something. It ends with a **question mark**. An exclamation is a sentence that shows strong feeling. It ends with an **exclamation mark**.

End Punctuation	
Period (.)	My name is Lisa.
Question Mark (?)	What would you like to eat?
Exclamation Mark (!)	Watch out for that car!

GO ON ▶

Name _____ Date _____

Skill Practice

1 **What is the BEST punctuation mark for the end of the sentence?**

Did you brush your teeth

  A a question mark

  B an exclamation point

  C a colon

  D a comma

2 **Which of the following is NOT a complete sentence?**

  A I met my friends at the soccer field.

  B Ask your mom if you can play with us.

  C The other team.

  D It started raining.

1 Ⓐ Ⓑ Ⓒ Ⓓ
2 Ⓐ Ⓑ Ⓒ Ⓓ

3 **What is the BEST punctuation mark for the end of the sentence?**

| A family of rabbits lives in our yard |

A a colon

B a question mark

C a comma

D a period

4 **Which of the following revisions makes the sentence complete?**

| Can help pick up trash. |

A We can help pick up trash.

B Picking up trash.

C Can help pick up trash!

D Recycling the trash.

5 **Which of the following is NOT a complete sentence?**

A We went there yesterday.

B The Taylors have four children.

C My arms hurt.

D The bird in the tree.

3 Ⓐ Ⓑ Ⓒ Ⓓ
4 Ⓐ Ⓑ Ⓒ Ⓓ
5 Ⓐ Ⓑ Ⓒ Ⓓ

GO ON ▶

6 **What is the BEST punctuation mark for
the end of the sentence?**

| This will be our best play ever |

A a question mark

B a comma

C an exclamation point

D a colon

7 **What is the BEST punctuation mark for
the end of the sentence?**

| I shared my lunch with the new boy |

A a question mark

B a comma

C a period

D an exclamation point

STOP

Context Clues

How to Analyze the Text

In *Diary of a Spider*, you may have seen some words you did not know. Perhaps you looked at the pictures to help you figure out the meaning. Perhaps you used **context clues** in nearby words and sentences.

Context clues are words that you <u>do</u> know that can help you figure out the meaning of words you <u>do not</u> know. Context clues might:

- **explain** the unknown word.
- give **examples** of the unknown word.
- **describe** the unknown word.

Let's see how it works. Read these examples.

Explain What words help to explain what <u>mallard</u> means?

The <u>mallard</u> chased us away from the pond. The mother duck didn't want us near her nest.

Examples What words are examples of what <u>urban</u> means?

Many ducks live in <u>urban</u> areas. They live in the parks found in cities and towns.

Describe What words help to describe what <u>reeds</u> means?

The nest was in the <u>reeds</u> by the pond. The nest was hard to see in the tall, thick grasses.

GO ON ▶

Apply to Text

Read the story. Then answer the questions.

The Mockingbird's Song

1   Once upon a time, none of
the birds in the world could
sing. This made the whole
world very sad. It also made
the world extremely quiet.

2   One day the Great Wise Bird decided
to make a change. He called all the birds
together. The Great Wise Bird said, "I will
give each of you a sweet song to sing.
Then you will be happy, and the world will
be a more joyful place."

3   All the birds were excited about the plan.
Each one wanted to be first in line. They
pushed and shoved to get the next song. One
bird was pushed so hard she fell out of the
tree. She tumbled into the tall grass below.
She was so scared that she could not move.

> **Look Closely**
>
> Look at the word <u>shoved</u>.
> What other words in
> Paragraph 3 help you figure
> out what <u>shoved</u> means?

4   Soon all of the birds had been given
melodies. The song of the crow was "caw,
caw." The song of the dove was "coo,
coo." The little sparrow sweetly sang,
"Tweet, tweet."

> **Look Closely**
>
> Which words help you
> understand what <u>melodies</u>
> are? Which words help you
> know what a <u>sparrow</u> is?

5   The little bird in the grass still had no
song. The Great Wise Bird looked down
and saw her.

6   "Little bird, you have waited a long time. I will give you a special gift," said the Great Wise Bird. "You may have part of each bird's song."

7   The little bird felt special. Now she could imitate any other bird. She could pretend to be any bird she wanted. This is why even today the mockingbird has so many songs.

1 **Which word in Paragraph 1 helps the reader know what the word <u>extremely</u> means?**

   A   made

   B   quiet

   C   sing

   D   very

Look Closely

Find the word <u>extremely</u> in Paragraph 1. Replace it with each answer choice. Which one makes sense in the sentence?

2 **What is the meaning of <u>joyful</u> in the sentence?**

> "Then you will be happy, and the world will be a more <u>joyful</u> place."

   A   very noisy

   B   full of birds

   C   full of joy, happy

   D   without any joy, sad

1 Ⓐ Ⓑ Ⓒ Ⓓ
2 Ⓐ Ⓑ Ⓒ Ⓓ

GO ON ▶

Name _____ Date _____

3 **Which words in the story help the
reader know what the word <u>shoved</u>
means?**

Look Closely

Reread Paragraph 3. Which
words are the best clues to
the meaning of <u>shoved</u>?

   A pushed so hard

   B could not move

   C get the next song

   D the tall grass below

4 **The meaning of the word <u>melodies</u> is**

> Soon all of the birds had been
> given <u>melodies</u>.

   A crow.

   B grass.

   C songs.

   D sweet.

Look Closely

Look back at the examples
given in Paragraph 4. Then
choose the correct definition
of <u>melodies</u>.

5 **Which words from the story help the
reader figure out the meaning of the
word <u>imitate</u>?**

   A felt special

   B pretend to be

   C so many songs

   D why even today

3 Ⓐ Ⓑ Ⓒ Ⓓ
4 Ⓐ Ⓑ Ⓒ Ⓓ
5 Ⓐ Ⓑ Ⓒ Ⓓ

STOP

Writing to Narrate

Overview

When you write a **narrative,** you write a story about what happens to a character. Sometimes you will be asked to write only an ending to a story.

Step 1: Plan Your Writing

Decide what you will write about. You might use a chart or web to help organize characters and events.

Step 2: Write a First Draft

Use your ideas to write a first draft. Introduce the story. Use details to describe events, characters, and feelings. Put events in the correct order. Write an ending.

Step 3: Revise Your Writing

When you **revise,** you make changes. You might add or take out words. You might add details. You might move sentences to put events in a better order. Maybe you need to add time order words such as <u>first</u>, <u>next</u>, <u>before</u>, and <u>then</u>.

Step 4: Edit Your Writing

Check your writing for errors in spelling or grammar. When you **edit,** you correct errors.

Step 5: Write a Final Draft

Write your final draft. As you write, make sure to include all your changes. Make sure the ending of your story makes sense. Use your best handwriting.

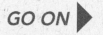
GO ON

Name _____ Date _____

Writing Practice

Read the text. Then follow the directions.

Pikey the Hedgehog

Mrs. Green's classroom was full of interesting things. Best of all was the class pet, Pikey the hedgehog.

Pikey had tiny black eyes and a nose that looked like a chocolate chip. His little mouth was always smiling. He was so cute! Pikey's cage was near Mrs. Green's desk. Inside were a food dish and a water bottle. Pikey ran on the wheel in his cage. He took a lot of naps.

One Monday morning, class began in the usual way. Students came into the room talking and laughing. Just as the bell rang, Maria looked at Pikey's cage. The door was open. There were small footprints near it. "Oh no!" she cried. "Pikey is missing!"

Write an ending to the story by adding details to tell what happens next. Use this space to help you plan your writing. Write your ending on your own sheet of paper.

_____

_____

STOP

Base Words and Prefixes

Skill Overview

You have read and heard the word <u>unhappy</u>. This word has two parts.

One part is called the **base word**. The base word is a word to which word parts can be added. The base word in <u>unhappy</u> is <u>happy</u>.

The other part is called the **prefix**. A prefix is a part of a word that can be put in front of a base word. The prefix changes the meaning of the base word. In the word <u>unhappy</u>, the prefix is *un-*. The prefix *un-* usually means "not," or "the opposite of."

Looking at a prefix and a base word can help you find out what a word means. Since *un-* means "not," the word <u>unhappy</u> means <u>not happy</u>, or <u>sad</u>.

Another common prefix is *re-*. The prefix *re-* usually means "again." If you <u>reread</u> a sentence in your book, you <u>read it again</u>. The base word in <u>reread</u> is <u>read</u>, and the prefix is *re-*.

If you know what prefixes mean, you can often figure out the meaning of words you may not know yet.

GO ON

Apply to Text

Read the story. Then answer the questions.

Setting the Table

1   "I'll set the table tonight," Jan told Mom. "I'll rewrite my story after dinner, so I have time."

Look Closely

What is the prefix in the word rewrite? What is the base word?

2   "That would be great!" Mom said. "Put the knife and the spoon on the right and the fork on the left. The napkins go under the forks, and the glasses go beside the plates."

3   "I won't forget," said Jan. She got three plates and put them on the table. Then she went to get the silverware. "Three knives, three forks, and three spoons," she said to herself. She went back to the table—and paused. Was it forks on the left, or forks on the right? Suddenly she was unsure.

Look Closely

What words do you see that have the prefixes re- and un-? What base words go with them?

4   Jan tried to think back to what Mom had said. "Oh, well," she said aloud. "If I get it wrong, I can redo it." She put the fork on the right and the knife and spoon on the left.

5   "Next, the napkins," said Jan, humming as she got them out of the cabinet.

The napkins were unfolded, so Jan
carefully folded them in half.

6   "Now where do the napkins go?" Jan
asked herself. What had Mom said? Jan
started to put the napkins under the forks,
but then she put the napkins above the
spoons instead.

7   "Next I'll get the glasses," Jan said to the
family dog, Spotty. But as she went into
the kitchen, Jan saw that her shoe was
untied. She quickly retied the laces. Then
she got three glasses from the kitchen.

8   "Where do the glasses go, Spotty?" she
asked. Spotty just wagged his tail. "You
are very unhelpful," said Jan. She decided
to put the glasses on top of the plates.
"I'm done!" Jan called to Mom.

9   "Great!" Mom called back. "Let me just
reheat the stew, and we'll be ready to eat!
Did you do a good job setting the table?"

10   Jan grinned and looked at her work. "I
did a great job!" she answered. "I didn't
forget a single thing that you said!"

Look Closely

If you know what tied means,
you can figure out untied
and retied by looking at the
prefixes.

Look Closely

What does the word unhelpful
mean? Look at the prefix and
the base word to find out.

GO ON ▶

1 In the story, Jan is <u>unsure</u> where to put the forks. What does this mean?

   A She knows where to put them.

   B She does not know where to put them.

   C She does not want to put the forks out.

   D She is planning to put the forks on the plates.

2 What is the meaning of the word <u>redo</u> in the story?

   A do something again

   B paint something red

   C do not do anything at all

   D say something for a second time

> **Look Closely**
> What is the base word in <u>redo</u>? What is the prefix?

3 Which word means the opposite of <u>tied</u>?

   A forgotten

   B retied

   C unfolded

   D untied

> **Look Closely**
> Which answer choice has the base word? Which answer choice has a prefix that means <u>the opposite of</u>?

4 Which word has a base word that means <u>to make hot</u> and a prefix that means <u>again</u>?

   A redo

   B reheat

   C rewrite

   D unhelpful

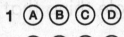
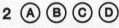

1 Ⓐ Ⓑ Ⓒ Ⓓ
2 Ⓐ Ⓑ Ⓒ Ⓓ
3 Ⓐ Ⓑ Ⓒ Ⓓ
4 Ⓐ Ⓑ Ⓒ Ⓓ

STOP

Writing and Research

Overview

Sometimes you will be asked to read two texts and then write to compare and contrast them. When you compare, you tell how things are alike. When you contrast, you tell how things are different.

Step 1: Plan Your Writing

Decide what you will write about. You might use a chart or web to help organize your ideas.

Step 2: Write a First Draft

Use your ideas to write a first draft. First, introduce the topic and texts. Then state your main ideas. Include facts and details from the two texts. Make sure your ideas are organized in a way that makes sense. Include an ending that sums up your ideas.

Step 3: Revise Your Writing

When you revise, you make changes. You might add or take out words. You might add details. You might move sentences to group ideas together. To compare ideas, you might use linking words such as <u>also</u> and <u>same</u>. To contrast, you might use <u>although</u>, <u>but</u>, <u>however</u>, or <u>instead</u>.

Step 4: Edit Your Writing

Check your writing for errors in spelling or grammar. When you edit, you correct errors.

Step 5: Write a Final Draft

Write your final draft. As you write, make sure to include all your changes. Make sure your conclusion sums up your ideas. Use your best handwriting.

GO ON

Name _____ Date _____

Writing Practice

Read the two texts that follow. Take notes on each one. After you read, follow the directions to write a paragraph about what you have read.

Powerful Foods

Eat your vegetables! You might hear this a lot. Well, it is good advice. Even the experts agree. Fruits and vegetables are packed with vitamins. Vitamins help you grow. They help you stay healthy.

Two important vitamins in these foods are vitamin A and vitamin C. Vitamin A helps fight off colds. It helps your eyes. Carrots and spinach have a lot of vitamin A. Oranges and sweet peppers have a lot of vitamin C. This vitamin helps your bones and teeth grow. It also helps your body heal.

About half the food you eat should be fruits and vegetables. You can eat these foods at every meal. They make great snacks. You can eat them fresh. They could be frozen and then warmed up. You can even make juice.

So the next time a parent serves you a fruit salad, don't complain. Dig in! Your body will thank you for it.

What are some reasons to eat fruits and vegetables?

Community Gardens

Community gardens are popular in many cities. Many people do not have yards. Instead, they work together in a neighborhood garden. Each family plants a section of the garden. Then they take care of their plants. Some families plant flowers or herbs. Others grow vegetables.

All summer, families watch their gardens grow. They water the plants and pull weeds. They watch the flowers bloom. Then they pick the vegetables. Some people will have fresh flowers in their houses. Others will enjoy fresh vegetables.

There are many reasons to have a community garden. It is a great place to make new friends. It gives a place to grow food and flowers. It lets people enjoy being outside. Community gardens make the city beautiful. Together with their friends and neighbors, community gardeners can make neighborhoods better.

What are reasons people work in a community garden?

_____

_____

GO ON ▶

Think about the ideas in the two texts you read. Write a paragraph about one idea that is the same in both texts. Use facts and details from both texts in your writing.

Use this space to plan your writing. Write your paragraph on your own sheet of paper.

_____

_____

_____

_____

_____

Cause and Effect

How to Analyze the Text

Often in a story, one event will cause another event to happen. The **cause** happens first. It tells why something happens. The **effect** is what happens because of that first event.

Cause (Why Something Happens)	Effect (What Happens)
It starts to rain.	People open their umbrellas.

You can look for clue words that tell about cause and effect. So, since, and because are all clue words that signal cause and effect. Look at these examples:

- I forgot my umbrella, <u>so</u> I got wet.

- <u>Since</u> I forgot my umbrella, I got wet.

- I got wet <u>because</u> I forgot my umbrella.

In each sentence, the cause is "I forgot my umbrella." The effect is "I got wet."

GO ON ▶

Apply to Text

Read the story. Then answer the questions.

Best Friends

1   Maya and Kathie were best friends. They were together a lot. If you saw one of the girls, you would probably see the other one, too.

2   But one day, Maya and Kathie had an argument on the playground at school. They were taking turns jumping rope. When it was Maya's turn, she tried to jump one hundred times without stopping.

3   Just as she got to ninety, though, Kathie bumped into her. Maya tripped over the rope and had to stop jumping. "You did that on purpose!" she said to Kathie.

> **Look Closely**
>
> What happens in Paragraph 3? What are the causes? What are the effects?

4   "I didn't," Kathie said. "Someone kicked a kickball near my head, so I moved fast. I didn't mean to get in your way."

> **Look Closely**
>
> According to Kathie, why did she step into Maya's way?

5   Maya didn't believe her. "You're just jealous because I'm better at jumping rope than you are," Maya snapped. "I don't want to be your friend anymore!"

> **Look Closely**
>
> Look for a word in Paragraph 5 that signals cause and effect.

6   That made Kathie feel angry. "Well, then, I won't be your friend either!" she said, stomping away.

7   At first, Maya felt happy that she and Kathie weren't best friends anymore. But then she began to change her mind. It wouldn't be as much fun riding her bike or going on her tire swing without Kathie.

Look Closely

What are some of the effects of Kathie getting angry?

8   "Look out!" someone yelled. Maya ducked as a kickball whizzed by her head!

9   "Hmm," Maya thought. "Maybe Kathie was telling the truth after all."

10   Maya found Kathie on the swings. "I'm sorry," Maya said. "I know you didn't mean to make me trip. Can we be friends again?"

11   Kathie smiled. "Sure," she said. "Why not?"

1 Why does Maya stop jumping after she jumps ninety times in a row? Give ONE detail from the story to support your answer.

_____

_____

_____

GO ON ▶

2 What happens when Maya says she doesn't want to be friends anymore? Give ONE detail from the story to support your answer.

_____

_____

_____

3 Complete the chart with ONE detail from the story.

Why It Happens	What Happens
_____	Maya ducks.

Explain why this detail accurately completes the chart. Use evidence from the text.

_____

_____

_____

STOP

Synonyms

Skill Overview

You already know that you can use context clues to help you figure out the meaning of a word. Context clues are words whose meanings you do know. They help to define, explain, or describe a word.

One kind of context clue is a synonym. A **synonym** is a word that means the same or almost the same as another word.

Think about the story *How Chipmunk Got His Stripes*. Remember how Brown Squirrel teased Bear? He said, "Bear is foolish. Bear is silly. Bear is stupid."

If you did not know the meaning of <u>foolish</u>, the synonyms <u>silly</u> and <u>stupid</u> could help you. The word <u>foolish</u> has the same or almost the same meaning as the words <u>silly</u> and <u>stupid</u>.

Read the examples below. Can you find the synonym for each underlined word?

Example Sentences	**Synonyms**
In first grade, I went to Sunshine Elementary. After we moved, I <u>attended</u> Orange Elementary.	attended = went to
Our new home has an <u>enormous</u> back yard. We can plant a garden in the big yard.	enormous = big
My little sister is an <u>infant</u>. She cries a lot because she is still a baby.	infant = baby

GO ON ▶

Apply to Text

Read the story. Then answer the questions that follow.

Guy Bluford

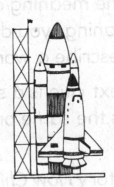

1   Guy Bluford always wanted
to fly. As a boy in the 1950s, he
liked to build model airplanes.
He also liked to assemble
model rockets. Guy's mother
was a teacher. His father was
an inventor. They wanted him
to do his best in school.

2   Guy liked math and science. He studied
rockets in college. After college, he was a
pilot in the Air Force. Guy was a very good
aviator. He taught many others how to fly.

3   In 1978, Guy started astronaut training.
He had 15 months of instruction. Finally,
Guy was picked to fly on the space shuttle
Challenger. He would be the first African
American to go into space. On August
30, 1983, Challenger was launched from
Kennedy Space Center in Florida.

4   Guy Bluford described what it was like to
be on the space shuttle. He said it was like
being in a giant elevator. While he was in
space, Guy assisted in many experiments.
He also helped put a satellite into space.

Look Closely

Find a word near assisted that
gives a clue to its meaning.

Name _____ Date _____

5   Guy Bluford went into space three more times. Each time he helped do more experiments. Guy spent over 688 hours in space.

6   Later he won many medals and awards for his work. In 2010, Guy was selected for the Astronaut Hall of Fame at Kennedy Space Center. Today, Guy sometimes visits schools and talks with students. He always tells them to work hard and do their best.

1   Which word from the passage means the SAME as the word <u>assemble</u> in the sentence above?

> He also liked to <u>assemble</u> model rockets.

   A build

   B inventor

   C model

   D wanted

> **Look Closely**
>
> Find this sentence in Paragraph 1. Look before and after the sentence for context clues.

2   Which words from the passage have almost the SAME meaning?

   A fly, space

   B pilot, aviator

   C giant, elevator

   D science, astronaut

1 Ⓐ Ⓑ Ⓒ Ⓓ
2 Ⓐ Ⓑ Ⓒ Ⓓ

GO ON ▶

3 **Which word from the passage is a synonym for the word <u>instruction</u>?**

> He had 15 months of <u>instruction</u>.

A astronaut

B shuttle

C space

D training

Look Closely

If you do not know which word to choose, try each one in the sentence. Choose the word that makes the most sense.

4 **Which word from the passage means almost the same as the word <u>assisted</u>?**

> While he was in space, Guy <u>assisted</u> in many experiments.

A described

B helped

C put

D said

Look Closely

Find this sentence in Paragraph 4. Now find another sentence in that paragraph that helps you know the meaning of <u>assisted</u>.

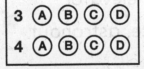

3 Ⓐ Ⓑ Ⓒ Ⓓ
4 Ⓐ Ⓑ Ⓒ Ⓓ

STOP

Writing to Inform

Overview

When you write to **inform**, you tell facts and details about something. You might explain how to do something. You might share information about a topic or explain how something works.

Step 1: Plan Your Writing

Decide on your topic. Write down your main idea and details. You might use a chart or a web to help you organize your thoughts.

Step 2: Write a First Draft

Use your ideas to write a first draft. First, introduce the topic. Then state your main points. Include facts, definitions, and details. Organize ideas in a way that makes sense. Include an ending that sums up your ideas.

Step 3: Revise Your Writing

When you **revise,** you make changes. You might add or take out words. You might add details. You might move sentences to group ideas together. Maybe you need to add linking words such as <u>first</u>, <u>next</u>, <u>before</u>, <u>because</u>, <u>finally</u>, and <u>then</u>. Linking words help connect ideas about a topic or steps in directions.

Step 4: Edit Your Writing

Check your writing for errors in spelling or grammar. When you **edit,** you correct errors.

Step 5: Write a Final Draft

Write your final draft. As you write, make sure to include all your changes. Make sure your conclusion sums up your ideas. Use your best handwriting.

GO ON ▶

Writing Practice

Read the text. Then follow the directions.

A Walk on the Beach

My sister and I were building a sand castle at the beach. We needed a seashell to finish off the top. We walked along the beach to find the perfect shell.

Seagulls flew in the air. They were calling out to each other. Soon we saw a pair of blue crabs digging in the sand. Far out in the water, we saw dolphins. They were diving in and out of the waves.

Up ahead, we saw baby turtles crawling into the water. I waded in the shallow water to keep looking. I found a beautiful starfish, but no shell.

We were about to give up. Suddenly my sister yelled, "Look!" I turned to see her holding up a perfect brown and white shell. We raced back to finish our sand castle.

In the story, the children see a lot of different animals. Think about an animal you have seen. Plan and write a paragraph to tell what you know about it. Write your paragraph on your own sheet of paper.

STOP

Name _____ Date _____

Language Arts

Skill Overview

A sentence is a group of words. Different kinds of words make up the parts of a sentence.

noun	names a person, animal, place or thing	The cat jumped.
verb	tells what people and animals do	The cat jumped.
pronoun	takes the place of a noun; includes the words he, she, it, you, we, and they, them	It jumped.
adjective	tells about a noun; may tell size, color, or how many	The big cat jumped.

The parts of a sentence must agree in number and time.

The cats are on the fence.   They are on the fence

Yesterday, the cat was on the fence.   Today, it is on the fence.

Capital letters help to make your writing clearer. Always use a capital letter to write the pronoun I. You should also use a capital letter to begin:

- each sentence

- the names of people, such as James Parker and Mr. Robinson

- the names of places, such as Atlanta and Main Street

- the names of days and months, such as Saturday and June

- the most important words in holidays, such as Cinco de Mayo

GO ON ▶

Name _____ Date _____

Skill Practice

1 **How should this sentence be written correctly?**

> My grandparents live near my uncle in macon.

A my grandparents live near my uncle in Macon.

B My grandparents live near my uncle in Macon.

C My grandparents live near my uncle in macon.

D my grandparents live near my uncle in macon.

2 **Which is the correct way to write the underlined words in the sentence?**

> The frog sat still, but then it jump away.

A it jumping

B it jumped

C they jump

D they had jumped

1 Ⓐ Ⓑ Ⓒ Ⓓ
2 Ⓐ Ⓑ Ⓒ Ⓓ

3 **Which is the correct way to write the underlined word in the sentence?**

> After the show, Mom carried my little sister to the <u>Car</u>.

A Cars

B Cares

C cars

D car

4 **Which is the correct way to write the underlined verb in the sentence?**

> I <u>has watered</u> the plant so that it will grow.

A waters

B will waters

C will has waters

D watered

5 **Which of the following words is a noun?**

> Ten clowns rode in a small red car.

A Ten

B clowns

C rode

D red

3 Ⓐ Ⓑ Ⓒ Ⓓ
4 Ⓐ Ⓑ Ⓒ Ⓓ
5 Ⓐ Ⓑ Ⓒ Ⓓ

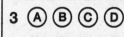

GO ON ▶

Name _____ Date _____

6 How should this sentence be written correctly?

"Surprise, amy! Happy birthday!" they called.

A "surprise, amy! Happy birthday!" they called.

B "Surprise, Amy! Happy birthday!" they called.

C "Surprise, amy! happy Birthday!" they called.

D "Surprise, Amy! Happy Birthday!" They called.

7 Which word is an adjective?

Ella's pink pencil is on the table in the kitchen.

A pink

B pencil

C table

D in

6 Ⓐ Ⓑ Ⓒ Ⓓ
7 Ⓐ Ⓑ Ⓒ Ⓓ

STOP ⬟

Text and Graphic Features
How to Analyze the Text

Ah, Music! has a **title** that tells about the topic. It has **headings** that tell what music is. It has **drawings** that help you understand what the author is writing about. Written words such as the title and headings are **text features**. Drawings are **graphic features**.

Read the chart to learn more about text and graphic features.

The **title** of a book or article usually tells the topic, or what the book or article is about.	**All Kinds of Cats**
The **author** is the name of the person who wrote the book.	*by Kitty B. Good*
A **heading** tells about the text that follows it. An author uses **special type** to stress a word. A bold word may be defined in the text.	**Where Lions Live** In the wild, lions live in open grasslands and savannas. A **savanna** is a hot, dry grassland with very few trees.
A drawing, photo, map or chart is a **graphic feature**. Graphic features tell more about the text. A **caption** is a word or group of words that tell more about a graphic feature.	A male lion has a mane. A **mane** is a growth of fur around the neck.

GO ON ▶

Name _____ Date _____

Apply to Text

Read the passage. Then answer the questions.

Sequoia National Park
by Everett Green

1   What is the heaviest living thing in the
world? Is it an elephant? Is it a blue whale?
No, it is a sequoia (suh KWOI uh) that
grows in Sequoia National Park. A sequoia
is a giant evergreen tree.

Giant Forest

2   California, or CA for short, is home to
Sequoia National Park. It is the second
oldest national park in America. One part
of this park is named the Giant Forest. It is
full of lovely meadows and giant sequoia
trees. These trees grow very tall. Many of
them are more than 300 feet tall! Sequoia
trees have bark the color of cinnamon
and their needles are green. They grow
pinecones in the shape of a chicken's egg!

General Sherman Tree

3   There is a very special tree in the Giant
Forest area. This tree is named the General
Sherman Tree. It is not the tallest tree. It
is not the widest tree. But it is the heaviest

tree. It weighs almost 3 million pounds.
That's about as heavy as forty huge trucks!
It is 275 feet tall. It is 30 feet across. It is
also more than two thousand years old.
The General Sherman Tree grows very,
very fast. Each year it adds enough wood
to build a two-bedroom home.

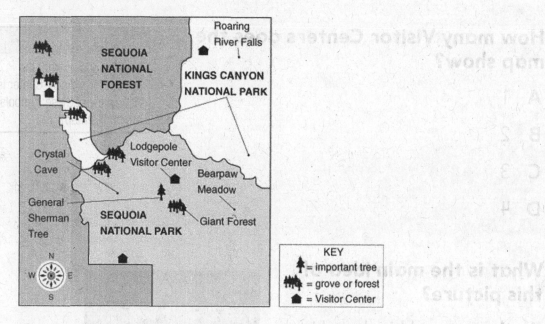

The compass rose helps you see the direction
you would travel to go from one place to another
in the park.

GO ON ▶

Name _____ Date _____

1 In which part of the passage are sequoia pinecones described?

A in the beginning paragraph

B in the map

C under the heading "Giant Forest"

D under the heading "General Sherman Tree"

2 How many Visitor Centers does the map show?

A 1

B 2

C 3

D 4

Look Closely

The Key shows what the symbol for a Visitor Center is. How many of these symbols are on the map?

3 What is the main idea of this picture?

A A man and his dog ski during the winter.

B A man and his dog hike in the mountains.

C A man and his dog run a road race.

D A man and his dog set up a campsite.

1 Ⓐ Ⓑ Ⓒ Ⓓ
2 Ⓐ Ⓑ Ⓒ Ⓓ
3 Ⓐ Ⓑ Ⓒ Ⓓ

STOP

Main Idea and Details

How to Analyze the Text

Every selection or story has a **main idea**. The main idea is what the selection or story is mostly about. In *Schools Around the World*, the main idea of the selection is that there are many kinds of schools around the world.

Each paragraph in a nonfiction selection has a main idea, too. It helps tell about the main idea of the whole selection.

Important details tell more about the main idea. They are sentences that answer questions such as <u>who</u>, <u>what</u>, <u>when</u>, <u>where</u>, <u>why</u>, and <u>how</u>.

Read this paragraph. Think about the main idea and the details.

> There are many expressions that compare people to animals. A person who swims well may "swim like a fish." Someone with many activities may be "as busy as a bee." A person who doesn't talk much may be "as quiet as a mouse." Someone who can run fast may be "as quick as a rabbit." What animal are you like?

You can list the main idea and details on a web. The main idea goes in the middle. The details go around the main idea. What details could you add to this web?

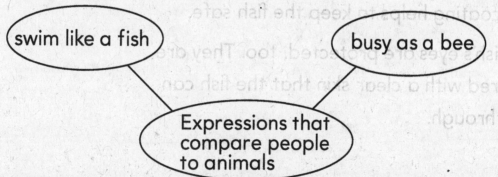

GO ON ▶

Apply to Text

Read the passage. Then answer the questions.

Just Like a Fish

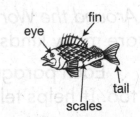

1   You might have heard someone say, "You swim like a fish." Are you really like a fish? Fish have many special parts that help them swim and live in the water.

2   Fish have fins. Fins are flaps that help a fish move through water. Fins also keep a fish straight in the water. Most fish have tail fins, too. They move the tail fin from side to side. This lets them push through the water.

3   Fish don't have lungs, as we do. They have gills to take oxygen from the water. Gills are openings on the sides of a fish's body. Gills help fish live in the water.

4   A fish's skin has scales. Scales are little bony plates that overlap each other. Fish have a slippery coating over their scales. The coating helps to keep the fish safe.

5   A fish's eyes are protected, too. They are covered with a clear skin that the fish can see through.

6   Most fish have skeletons made of bone.
Their skeletons are able to bend and twist.
This helps fish swim through water.

7   Fish also have a special shape. They
are pointed at the front and wider at the
center. This shape lets them move through
water easily.

8   You really aren't very much like a fish,
are you?

**1 What is the main idea of the whole passage? Give
TWO details from the passage to support your
answer.**

_____

_____

_____

_____

GO ON ▶

2 **What is Paragraph 4 mainly about? Give TWO details from the passage to support your answer.**

_____

_____

_____

3 **Complete the web with THREE details from the passage.**

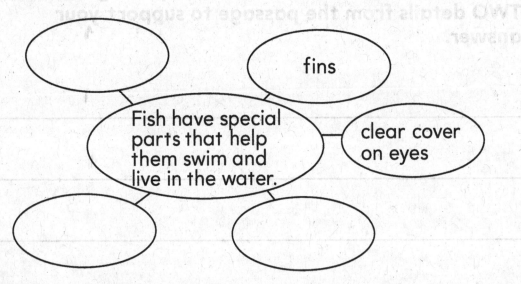

fins

clear cover on eyes

Fish have special parts that help them swim and live in the water.

Explain why these details accurately complete the chart.

_____

_____

_____

STOP

Suffixes

Skill Overview

A **suffix** is a word part that is added to the end of a word. A suffix has a meaning all its own. When a suffix is added to a base word, it changes the meaning of the base word.

The chart below lists the meanings of some common suffixes.

Suffix	Meaning	Example
-y	"being or having"	flowery (being like a flower) rainy (having rain)
-ly	"in a way that is"	quickly (in a way that is quick) warmly (in a way that is warm)
-ful	"full of"	cheerful (full of cheer) playful (full of play)

When you read an unknown word, look to see if it has a suffix. If it does, look at the base word. Think about its meaning and then think about the meaning of the suffix. Then think about how the suffix changes the meaning of the base word.

GO ON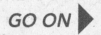

Apply to Text

Read the story. Then answer the questions.

Mail for Danny

1   Every day Danny watched his parents
open their mail. "Is there any
mail for me?" Danny would ask.

2   "No," said his father and
mother, "not today."

3   "I never get any mail," Danny
said sadly.

4   One sunny day, Danny's
mother found some postcards in a drawer.
She showed them to Danny and said, "If you
want to get mail, you should try writing to
someone first. If you are lucky, that person
will write back."

5   Danny was hopeful. "I could send this
postcard of the Memphis Zoo to Kim. She
wants to see it when she comes to visit with
Uncle Jack this summer."

6   Danny wrote neatly on the postcard, "Hi
Kim. Here is a picture of the elephants at
the Memphis Zoo. We will see them when
you come to visit. We can go to the petting
zoo, too! Bring old clothes, though, because
you might get dirty! Your Cousin, Danny."

7   Mom was helpful. She wrote Uncle Jack's
address on the postcard. Then they put a
stamp on the postcard and mailed it.

> **Look Closely**
>
> The base word sad means
> "not happy." Think about
> how the suffix -ly changes its
> meaning.

8   Danny checked the mail each day. Finally, after a week, he cried out, "Mom, I have mail! It's a postcard from Kim with a picture of Centennial Olympic Park. Kim says we can visit it when we go to Atlanta!"

1 In the sentence, the word <u>sadly</u> means

> "I never get any mail," Danny said <u>sadly</u>.

A not sad.

B full of sad.

C in a way that is sad.

D being or having sad.

Look Closely

Think about how the suffix *-ly* changes the meaning of the word. Then choose the answer that has the same meaning as the word <u>sadly</u> in Paragraph 3.

2 What is the meaning of the word <u>lucky</u> in the sentence?

> "If you are <u>lucky</u>, that person will write back."

A bad luck

B having luck

C without luck

D in a way that is luck

1 Ⓐ Ⓑ Ⓒ Ⓓ
2 Ⓐ Ⓑ Ⓒ Ⓓ

3 **In the sentence, the word <u>hopeful</u> means**

Danny was <u>hopeful</u>.

A like hope.

B full of hope.

C without hope.

D with a little hope.

4 **In the sentence, the word <u>dirty</u> means**

Bring old clothes, though, because you might
get <u>dirty</u>!

A having dirt.

B without dirt.

C not like dirt.

D in a way that is dirt.

5 **What is the meaning of the word <u>helpful</u> in the sentence?**

Mom was <u>helpful</u>.

A no help

B like help

C not helping

D full of help

3 Ⓐ Ⓑ Ⓒ Ⓓ
4 Ⓐ Ⓑ Ⓒ Ⓓ
5 Ⓐ Ⓑ Ⓒ Ⓓ

STOP ⬣

Writing Opinions

Overview

When you write an **opinion,** you tell what you think about a topic. You give reasons to support your opinion.

Step 1: Plan Your Writing

To begin, you might make a list of topics or ideas. Circle the one you want to write about. You might use a chart or web to help you organize your thoughts.

Step 2: Write a First Draft

Use your ideas to write a first draft. It does not have to be perfect. First, write a main sentence that tells your opinion. Then write sentences that give reasons that support your opinion. Write a conclusion that restates your opinion.

Step 3: Revise Your Writing

When you **revise,** you make changes. You might add or take out words. You might add details. You might move sentences to put events in a better order. Maybe you need to add linking words such as <u>because</u> or <u>also</u>. Linking words help connect your opinion with your reasons.

Step 4: Edit Your Writing

Check your writing for errors in spelling or grammar. When you **edit,** you correct errors.

Step 5: Write a Final Draft

Write your final draft. As you write, make sure to include all of your changes. Make sure you have a conclusion. Use your best handwriting.

GO ON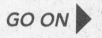

Writing Practice

Read the text. Then follow the directions.

Highbridge Elementary School Rules

- Listen to all of your teachers.
- Raise your hand to speak.
- Do not damage school property.
- Do not interrupt others when they are speaking.
- Take care of books and other classroom items.
- Keep your hands and feet to yourself.
- Do not run or race between classrooms.
- Arrive at school promptly at 8:00 a.m. each day.
- Do not use the playground without adult supervision.
- Strive to do your best at all times!

Which rule above do you think is the most important? Write your opinion in a paragraph. Give reasons.

Use this space to help you plan your writing. Write your opinion paragraph on your own sheet of paper.

_____

_____

STOP

Story Structure

How to Analyze the Text

When you draw a house, you include parts so that your picture makes sense and people know what it is. The picture includes things like walls, a roof, windows, and a door.

A story also needs certain parts in order to make sense. These story parts help answer the questions <u>who</u>, <u>where</u>, <u>when</u>, and <u>what</u>. Read the chart to learn about the different story parts.

Story Questions	Story Part
<u>Who</u> is in the story?	The **characters** are the people or the animals in the story.
<u>Where</u> does the story take place? <u>When</u> does the story take place?	The **setting** is the time and place where the story happens.
<u>What</u> happens in the story? <u>What</u> is the story problem?	The **plot** is the series of events that happen in the story. The beginning usually tells about a problem the character has. The middle tells how the character tries to solve the problem. The ending tells how the problem is solved.

Think about *Mr. Tanen's Tie Trouble*. Can you name the characters, setting, and plot for this story?

GO ON ▶

Apply to Text

Name _____ Date _____

Read the story. Then answer the questions.

Roberto's Rainbow

1   Roberto was very excited. He had been saving his money to buy a kite, and today he was going to get one.

2   Roberto and his sister went to the toy store. There were too many kites to choose from!

3   "Look at this blue kite, Roberto! It's your favorite color," said his sister.

4   Roberto looked at the blue kite and nodded, "It's as blue as the sky outside."

5   He picked up the blue kite and walked toward the counter. Halfway there, he stopped. "Do I really want this kite?" he asked himself. He walked back to the kites and put down the blue kite. Next, he picked up a yellow one.

6   "This one looks like the bright morning sun," he thought to himself.

7   Just then, he saw a bright red kite. It made Roberto think of tasty tomatoes.

8   "What's taking you so long?" Roberto's sister asked.

9   "The blue kite reminds me of the sky outside. The yellow kite looks like the bright sun. The reddish kite looks like the tomatoes on Papa's farm. I don't know which kite to choose. I like them all," Roberto explained.

10   Just then Roberto's sister held up a kite that looked like a rainbow. This kite had everything—bits of blue, yellow, and red. It also had stripes of green, orange, and purple. It was perfect!

11   Roberto ran to pay the clerk for his new kite. He couldn't wait to fly it.

1   Who is the MAIN character in the story? How do you know? Use evidence from the text to support your answer.

_____

_____

_____

GO ON ▶

2 Where does the story take place? Use evidence from the text to support your answer.

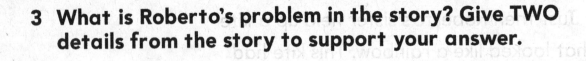

_____

_____

_____

3 What is Roberto's problem in the story? Give TWO details from the story to support your answer.

_____

_____

_____

4 How is the problem solved? Use evidence from the text to support your answer.

_____

_____

_____

STOP

Writing and Research

Overview

Sometimes you will be asked to read two texts and then write to compare and contrast them. When you compare, you tell how things are alike. When you contrast, you tell how things are different.

Step 1: Plan Your Writing

Decide what you will write about. You might use a chart or web to help organize your ideas.

Step 2: Write a First Draft

Use your ideas to write a first draft. First, introduce the topic and texts. Then state your main ideas. Include facts and details from the two texts. Make sure your ideas are organized in a way that makes sense. Include an ending that sums up your ideas.

Step 3: Revise Your Writing

When you **revise,** you make changes. You might add or take out words. You might add details. To compare ideas, you might use linking words such as <u>also</u> and <u>same</u>. To contrast, you might use <u>although</u>, <u>but</u>, <u>however</u>, or <u>instead</u>.

Step 4: Edit Your Writing

Check your writing for errors in spelling or grammar. When you **edit,** you correct errors.

Step 5: Write a Final Draft

Write your final draft. Make sure to include all your changes. Make sure your conclusion sums up your ideas. Use your best handwriting.

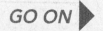

GO ON

Writing Practice

Read the two texts that follow. Take notes on each one. After you read, follow the directions to write a paragraph about what you have read.

J. K. Rowling

J. K. Rowling is one of the most famous authors in the world. Children and adults love her books about Harry Potter. But success did not come easily.

Rowling knew her idea for the story of Harry Potter was a good one. But writing the book was difficult. She did not have a job or much money. It took her five years to finish the book.

Rowling was proud of her book. She took it to a publisher, but the publisher did not like it. This happened many times. But she would not quit. It took her a year, but Rowling finally found a publisher that loved her writing and published Harry Potter and the Sorcerer's Stone.

Rowling wrote six more Harry Potter books. The seven books have been published in 60 different languages and made into movies. J. K. Rowling is a huge success story.

What problems did J. K. Rowling have while writing her book?

Bethany Hamilton

Bethany Hamilton was born in Hawaii. She began surfing when she was 4 years old. At age 8, she won her first surfing competition. She entered and won many more competitions.

One day when Bethany was 13, she went surfing as usual. A shark attacked her! The shark bit off most of her left arm. Bethany was rushed to the hospital. The doctors saved her life. But they could not save her arm.

After the attack, Bethany had to learn how to do things with just one arm. Simple tasks were now difficult. But one month after the attack, she was back in the water. Her dad invented a special handle for her surfboard. It helped her control the board with only one hand. Soon she was surfing again.

One year later, Bethany was competing again. In 2004, she won the Teen Choice Courage Award. The story of her life was made into a movie. Bethany Hamilton showed the world that hard work helps you reach your goals.

What are some ways Bethany overcame difficulties?

_____

_____

GO ON ▶

Name _____ Date _____

Think about the two texts you have read. Write a paragraph to explain how J. K. Rowling and Bethany Hamilton proved that hard work can lead to success. Use facts and details from both texts in your writing.

Use this space to plan your writing. Write your paragraph on your own sheet of paper.

_____

_____

_____

_____

STOP

Poetry

How to Analyze the Text

A poem uses words in a special way to tell about something. Poems often use details that help the reader paint a picture in his or her head. Authors do this by using words about the five senses. They tell how something looks, smells, tastes, feels, or sounds. Some poems have rhyming words; some use rhythm.

A poem can describe something. It can also tell a story. In a story poem, there can be characters. Characters are the people in a story. They can be fictional people, like Gabriela in the story *My Name Is Gabriela*. They can also be real people.

Knowing about characters will help you understand a poem or story. Ask yourself questions like the ones below to help you learn more about a character.

- How does the character act?

- What does the character say?

- How does the character treat other people?

- How does the character change?

GO ON ▶

Name _____ Date _____

Apply to Text

Read the poem. Then answer the questions.

1   We woke up at the crack of dawn

     to do a special deed.

     We're picking lots of oranges

     for people with a need.

5   The oranges are large and curved,

     just like a basketball!

     We pull them off the tree just as

     they're ripe enough to fall.

     We drop them in a wooden box.

10   They go plop, plop, plop, plop!

     We've got a ton of oranges!

     Our job will never stop.

     They taste like bits of sunshine,

     so pretty and so round.

15   Maybe I will keep the seeds

     and plant them in the ground.

     We pick together side by side.

     It's quite a sight to see.

Look Closely

Does this poem use rhyme? How can you tell?

Name _____ Date _____

All our hands and many more

20   help children just like me!

One time the wind picked up.

It blew right through the trees.

The branches danced like ballerinas

Swaying in the breeze.

25   Besides the pails of oranges,

we picked some nuts to munch.

Some other people cooked some soup.

We made a tasty lunch!

Today a bunch of neighbors

30   took time out from their play.

We worked to feed the hungry.

It was a special day!

Look Closely

Based on what they do, what can you tell about the characters in the poem?

1 **Who are the characters in the poem picking oranges for?**

  A themselves

  B people in need

  C farmers

  D adults

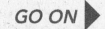

GO ON ▶

Name _____ Date _____

2 How does the narrator feel at the end of the poem?

Look Closely

Think about the words the narrator uses to describe picking oranges.

A happy

B sad

C hungry

D sleepy

3 Which word BEST describes the narrator?

A angry

B selfish

C handsome

D generous

4 To what are the characters in the poem comparing oranges?

A a wooden box

B ballerinas

C a basketball

D a big tree

2 Ⓐ Ⓑ Ⓒ Ⓓ
3 Ⓐ Ⓑ Ⓒ Ⓓ
4 Ⓐ Ⓑ Ⓒ Ⓓ

STOP

Text and Graphic Features

Skill Overview

In the story *The Signmaker's Assistant*, signs are an important part of the story. If you did not look at the illustrations and did not read the signs, it would be hard to understand the story.

Authors use **graphic features** to tell more about a story or topic. Graphic features include drawings, photographs, maps, charts, and signs. Graphic features add details and show information about a topic.

Authors also use **text features** to give information. Text features can be headings, captions, or lists. Or, authors may make text stand out in boldface, italics, or large type. Text features help readers pay attention to important words or ideas.

Look for text and graphic features below. How do they help readers?

ASK THE PLANT MAN!	
Dear Plant Man, Under my pine tree, there are pinecones everywhere. What are they for? —Luke Higgins, Age 7	**Life Cycle of a Pine Tree** 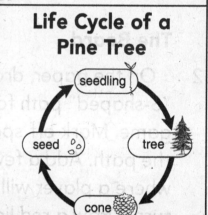

Dear Luke,
    A pinecone is a cluster of scales with many seeds. When a pinecone falls off a tree, some of the seeds start growing in the ground. These baby plants are called seedlings. A seedling grows into a new pine tree.
 	
                        —The Plant Man
	Pine trees make cones full of seeds. Seedlings grow into new pine trees.

GO ON ▶

Name _____ Date _____

Apply to Text

Read the instructions. Then answer the questions.

Making a Board Game

1   It's a rainy day outside. You and a friend are stuck in the house. What can you do? Make your own board game!

For the game board, you will need:

- Construction paper

- Pencil or marker

For the spinner, you will need:

- Piece of cardboard

- Straw

- Pin

Look Closely
Text features present information in an organized way. What information do these lists give you?

The Board

2   On the paper, draw an "S-shaped" path for your game. Mark off spaces on the path. Add a few spaces where a player will lose a turn. Draw a red light or a STOP sign on these spaces. Add a few spaces where a player gets an extra turn. Draw a star or a green light on these spaces. Include a <u>Start</u> and a <u>Finish</u>.

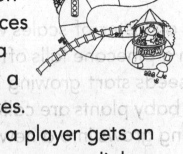

The Spinner

3   Next, make a spinner.
Draw a circle on the
cardboard. Mark the spinner
to show how many spaces a
player will move. Cut a straw
to be the pointer. Stick a pin through one
end of the pointer and then push it into
the cardboard. Hold the pin with one hand.
Flick the straw with a finger. If the straw
lands on a line, spin again.

The Playing Pieces

4   Choose two playing pieces. Dry beans or
coins work well. You may also use pieces
from another game, like checkers. Be sure
to put them back when you are done.

The Rules

5   Now make the rules for your game. Write
them down. Be sure the rules are fair. Have
fun!

**1 What information can you find in the lists in
    Paragraph 1?**

    A game rules

    B supplies needed

    C game piece ideas

    D how to make the spinner

Name _____ Date _____

2 Under which heading can you find the kinds of spaces to draw?

A "The Board"

B "The Spinner"

C "The Playing Pieces"

D "The Rules"

3 What information does the graphic next to the heading "The Board" give?

A It shows how to win the game.

B It shows the words <u>Start</u> and <u>Finish</u>.

C It shows what kind of game pieces you must use.

D It shows what part of the game board might look like.

4 How many spaces would a player move if the player made the spin shown on the spinner?

A 1 space

B 2 spaces

C 3 spaces

D 4 spaces

2 (A) (B) (C) (D)

3 (A) (B) (C) (D)

4 (A) (B) (C) (D)

Writing to Narrate

Overview

When you write a **narrative,** you might write about what happens to a character. Sometimes you will be asked to write about a special person or an event in your life.

Step 1: Plan Your Writing

Decide who or what you will write about. You might use a chart or web to organize ideas and details about your subject.

Step 2: Write a First Draft

Use your ideas to write a first draft. Introduce the story. Use details to describe events, characters, and feelings. Put events in the correct order. Write an ending.

Step 3: Revise Your Writing

When you **revise,** you make changes. You might add or take out words. You might add details. You might move sentences to put events in a better order. Maybe you need to add linking words such as <u>when</u>, <u>before</u>, <u>because</u>, and <u>then</u>.

Step 4: Edit Your Writing

Check your writing for errors in spelling or grammar. When you **edit,** you correct errors.

Step 5: Write a Final Draft

Write your final draft. As you write, make sure to include all of your changes. Make sure the ending of your story makes sense. Use your best handwriting.

GO ON

Writing Practice

Read the text. Then follow the directions.

Buddy's Hero

Last weekend my dad and I went hiking with our dog Buddy. We chose the path by the river.

Suddenly I heard a big splash. Buddy had fallen in the river! The current was strong, and Buddy was struggling to keep his head up. The riverbank was too steep for us to get to Buddy right away, so I yelled for help.

All of a sudden, I saw a man jump into the water and swim toward Buddy. I could see that it was difficult to swim against the current. But the man reached Buddy and grabbed him by his collar. Then they swam back to shore.

My dad and I scrambled down the riverbank as quickly as we could. When we got to the shore, Buddy ran right over to me. I gave him a big hug. Then I ran over to the man.

"Thank you for saving my dog," I said. "You are my hero!"

Plan and write a paragraph about someone you know who is your hero. Include details. Write your paragraph on your own sheet of paper.

STOP

Main Idea and Details

How to Analyze the Text

Every selection has a **main idea**. The main idea is what the selection is mostly about. In *Penguin Chicks*, the main idea of the selection is how baby penguins hatch and grow.

A paragraph can have a main idea, too. It can help to tell about the main idea of the whole selection.

Sometimes a main idea is clearly stated. At other times, you must work harder to find it. **Important details** can help you figure out the main idea. They answer questions such as <u>who</u>, <u>what</u>, <u>when</u>, <u>where</u>, <u>why</u>, and <u>how</u>.

When you think about a main idea and details, think about a table. The main idea is the tabletop. The important details are the legs. They support the main idea.

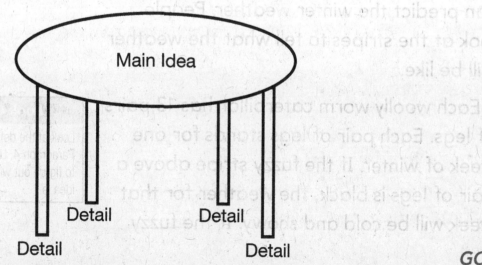

GO ON ▶

Apply to Text

Read the passage. Then answer the questions.

Woolly Worm Festival

1   Every fall, some towns in the United States have a woolly worm festival. The people in the town hold a special race. It is not just any race. They race woolly worms!

2   Woolly worms are not real worms. They are caterpillars. The brown and black hairs on their fuzzy bodies form stripes. Sometimes these furry insects are called "woolly bears." Isn't that a strange name for caterpillars that will someday turn into tiger moths?

3   Why are these caterpillars so special? Some people think that the woolly worms can predict the winter weather. People look at the stripes to tell what the weather will be like.

4   Each woolly worm caterpillar has 13 pairs of legs. Each pair of legs stands for one week of winter. If the fuzzy stripe above a pair of legs is black, the weather for that week will be cold and snowy. If the fuzzy

Look Closely

Look at the details in Paragraph 4. Use the details to figure out what the main idea is.

Name _____ Date _____

stripe is brown, the weather will be mild
with little snow.

5   What is a woolly worm race like? Well,
when the race begins, each caterpillar is
put on the bottom of its string. The first
caterpillar to climb to the top is the winner.
The person with the winning worm gets a
prize. Then the winning worm is used to
predict the weather!

**1 What is the main idea of the whole passage? Give
TWO details from the passage to support your
answer.**

_____

_____

_____

**2 What is Paragraph 3 mainly about? Give TWO
details from the passage to support your answer.**

_____

_____

_____

GO ON ▶

3 Complete the web with TWO details about woolly worms from the passage.

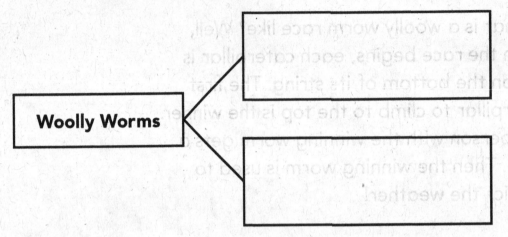

Woolly Worms

Explain why these details accurately complete the web.

_____

_____

_____

STOP

Language Arts

Skill Overview

A **pronoun** is a part of speech. It takes the place of a noun. Common pronouns are: <u>he</u>, <u>she</u>, <u>it</u>, <u>they</u>, and <u>us</u>. When writing pronouns in sentences, be sure that they stand for the noun or pronouns correctly.

The boy is here.　　　*He* is here.

Verb tense tells when an action happens: in the present (happens now), past (happened before), or future (will happen later).

Present Tense	Past Tense	Future Tense
The children <u>sing</u>.	We <u>sang</u>.	We <u>will sing</u>.
The dogs <u>run</u>.	They <u>ran</u>.	They <u>will run</u>.
My dad <u>paints</u>.	He <u>painted</u>.	He <u>will paint</u>.

Commas have many purposes in writing. One way commas are used is to separate words in a series.

Incorrect	Correct
We ate eggs toast and fruit.	We ate eggs, toast, and fruit.

You can improve your spelling by using spelling rules. One spelling rule is that when a word ends in a consonant-vowel-consonant (CVC) pattern, you double the final consonant before adding an –*ed*, –*ing*, or –*er*.

step + ed	stepped	let + ing	letting	big + er	bigger

GO ON ▶

Skill Practice

Read and answer the questions.

1 Choose the sentences that use pronouns correctly.

A First Owen walked his dog. Then it cleaned his room.

B First Owen walked his dog. Then she cleaned his room.

C First Owen walked his dog. Then he cleaned his room.

D First Owen walked his dog. Then we cleaned his room.

2 What is the correct spelling for the underlined word?

> Mike <u>grabed</u> the ball and ran.

A grabedd

B grabet

C grabbed

D grab

3 Which sentence uses commas correctly?

A We should stop, look and listen,
before crossing the street.

B We should stop, look, and listen,
before crossing the street.

C We should stop look and listen
before crossing the street.

D We should stop, look, and listen
before crossing the street.

1 Ⓐ Ⓑ Ⓒ Ⓓ
2 Ⓐ Ⓑ Ⓒ Ⓓ
3 Ⓐ Ⓑ Ⓒ Ⓓ

STOP

Sequence of Events

How to Analyze the Text

In a story, the author usually tells events in the order in which they happen. An author tells what happens first, what happens next, and what happens last. This order is called the **sequence of events**. Understanding the sequence of events helps the story make sense.

Time-order words can help you figure out the sequence of events. Time-order words include:

- *today, yesterday*
- *first, next, then, last*
- *after, before*
- *finally, later*

In *The Goat in the Rug*, the author tells events in the order they happen: First, Glenmae clips off Geraldine's wool. Next Glenmae washes, dries, and combs the wool. After that, she spins the wool into yarn. Then she dyes the yarn. Finally, Glenmae weaves the yarn to make a rug.

A flowchart, like this one, can help keep track of the sequence of events in a story.

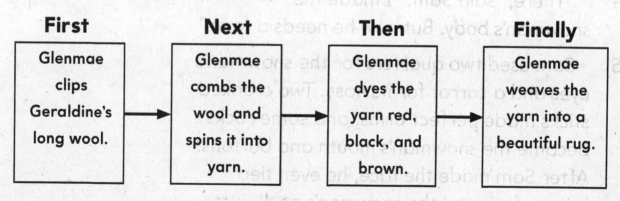

First	**Next**	**Then**	**Finally**
Glenmae clips Geraldine's long wool.	Glenmae combs the wool and spins it into yarn.	Glenmae dyes the yarn red, black, and brown.	Glenmae weaves the yarn into a beautiful rug.

GO ON ▶

Apply to Text

Read the story. Then answer the questions.

The Snowman's Cap

1   Snow fell softly all through the night. By morning, it lay deep on the icy ground. When Sam woke up, he rubbed his eyes and looked out the window. "Snow!" he cried. "I can build a snowman."

2   After breakfast, Sam got dressed in his warm winter clothes. "Don't forget your scarf," said his mother. She wrapped the red and white scarf around Sam's neck and tied it. "Have fun building your snowman."

3   First, Sam rolled a snowball in the snow. Sam rolled and rolled it until he made a great big ball. Next he made another one not quite as big and put it atop the first ball. Then he made a ball the size of a melon and set it atop the other two.

4   "There," said Sam. "I made the snowman's body. But now he needs a face."

5   Sam used two quarters for the snowman's eyes and a carrot for its nose. Two crooked sticks made perfect arms, and some rocks became the snowman's mouth and buttons. After Sam made the face, he even tied his scarf around the snowman's neck, just as Mom did for Sam. The snowman was

Name _____ Date _____

looking pretty good.

6 "It needs one more thing," said Sam. He thought of his dad's favorite baseball cap. It was bright red, the same shade of red that was in Sam's scarf. Sam was sure his dad would let him borrow the cap, just for today.

7 "There," said Sam, putting the cap on the snowman's head. "I finally finished my snowman. Now it looks great!"

1 When does Sam get dressed in his winter clothes?

   A after breakfast

   B after he went outside

   C after he made his snowman

   D after Mom gave him his scarf

> **Look Closely**
>
> Look back at the beginning of the story. When does Sam put on his winter clothes?

2 What is the FIRST thing Sam does to build his snowman?

   A He finds two sticks.

   B He borrows Dad's favorite cap.

   C He rolls a snowball in the snow.

   D He makes the snowman's face and arms.

1 Ⓐ Ⓑ Ⓒ Ⓓ
2 Ⓐ Ⓑ Ⓒ Ⓓ

GO ON ▶

3 **What does Sam do AFTER he makes the snowman's face?**

A   He finds some rocks.

B   He puts his scarf on the snowman.

C   He rolls three big snowballs in the snow.

D   He uses a carrot to make the snowman's nose.

4 **Lisa made this chart after reading the story.**

1. Sam makes the snowman's body.
2. Sam makes the snowman's face.
3.
4. Sam finally finishes his snowman and thinks it looks great.

Which event belongs in the empty space?

A   Sam rolls three big snowballs.

B   Sam goes inside to eat breakfast.

C   Sam puts his mittens on the snowman.

D   Sam borrows Dad's cap for the snowman.

3 Ⓐ Ⓑ Ⓒ Ⓓ
4 Ⓐ Ⓑ Ⓒ Ⓓ

STOP

Cause and Effect

How to Analyze the Text

You may remember that one event in a story can cause another event to happen. The **cause** happens first. It tells why something happens. The **effect** is what happens because of that first event.

Example: *Jonah slams the door loudly. The baby wakes up.*

Cause (Why Something Happens)	Effect (What Happens)
Jonah slams the door loudly.	The baby wakes up.

Sometimes a cause can lead to more than one effect. Think about the story *Half-Chicken*. A mother hen has a very unusual chick. What are the effects of the way the chick looks?

Cause (Why Something Happens)	Effect (What Happens)
The thirteenth chick has only one wing, one leg, and one eye.	1. Everyone calls him Half-Chicken. 2. He becomes the center of attention.

What other effects happened because Half-Chicken had only one wing, one leg, and one eye?

GO ON

Apply to Text

Read the story. Then answer the questions.

The Lion and the Mouse

1   One day, a tiny mouse was running through the jungle. She was in such a hurry to get home, she tripped over the tail of a sleeping lion.

2   Before the mouse could get up, the lion had her under his paw. He roared, "Since you woke me up, I'm going to eat you!"

3   "Please don't eat me," the mouse squealed. "My family needs me. If you set me free, I promise that when you need help, I will show you kindness, too."

4   "A little mouse like you, help me?" the lion laughed. "Since you made me laugh, I will let you go. Besides, your family needs you more than I need a snack."

Look Closely

What effect do the mouse's words have on the lion?

5   "Oh, thank you," cried the mouse. "You won't be sorry!"

6   A few days later, terrible roars filled the air, so the jungle animals hid in their homes. Only the little mouse was brave enough to see what the trouble was. She

hurried through the bushes and found the lion caught in a net!

7   "Now you will see that I can help!" the mouse said. She quickly began to chew on the net. Bit by bit, the ropes fell away. Soon the lion was free!

8   "Thank you," the lion said. "You were right. Even a small friend can be a great help."

1 What happens to wake up the lion?

   A The lion is hungry.

   B The lion hears a roar.

   C The mouse has a family.

   D The mouse trips on the lion's tail.

Look Closely

Think about cause and effect. The effect is that the lion wakes up. What is the cause?

2 Why does the lion let the mouse go?

   A The lion is not hungry.

   B The mouse is too small.

   C The mouse makes the lion laugh.

   D The lion wants to go back to sleep.

1 Ⓐ Ⓑ Ⓒ Ⓓ

2 Ⓐ Ⓑ Ⓒ Ⓓ

GO ON ▶

Name _____ Date _____

3 Why does the mouse thank the lion?

A The lion lets her go.

B The lion says she is funny.

C The lion gives her a snack.

D The lion knows her family.

Look Closely

"Why" asks about the cause of an event. What happened to make the mouse thank the lion?

4 Which event does NOT happen because the lion is caught in a net?

A Terrible roars fill the air.

B The animals hide in their homes.

C Bushes grow in the jungle.

D The mouse goes to see what the trouble is.

5 Ryan made this chart after reading the story.

Why It Happens	What Happens
	The lion is set free.

Which cause belongs in the empty box?

A The animals help the lion.

B The mouse chews through the net.

C The jungle animals hide in their homes.

D The little mouse runs through the bushes.

3 Ⓐ Ⓑ Ⓒ Ⓓ
4 Ⓐ Ⓑ Ⓒ Ⓓ
5 Ⓐ Ⓑ Ⓒ Ⓓ

STOP

Name _____ Date _____

Writing to Inform

Overview

When you write to **inform,** you tell facts and details about something. You might explain how to do something. You might share information about a topic or explain how something works.

Step 1: Plan Your Writing

Decide on your topic. Write down the necessary steps and details. You might use a chart or a web to organize the steps in the correct order.

Step 2: Write a First Draft

Use your ideas to write a first draft. First, introduce the topic. When writing directions, you may want to put steps in a numbered list. Organize the steps in a way that makes sense. Write an ending that sums up your topic.

Step 3: Revise Your Writing

When you **revise,** you make changes. You might add or take out words. You might add details. You might move sentences to put steps in the correct order. Maybe you need to add linking words such as <u>first</u>, <u>next</u>, <u>before</u>, <u>finally</u>, and <u>then</u>. Linking words help connect ideas about a topic or steps in directions.

Step 4: Edit Your Writing

Check your paper for errors in spelling or grammar. When you **edit,** you correct errors.

Step 5: Write a Final Draft

Write your final draft. As you write, make sure to include all of your changes. Use your best handwriting.

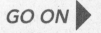
GO ON

Writing Practice

Read the text. Then follow the directions.

How to Plant a Garden

People everywhere plant gardens. Read to find out how you can plant your very own garden.

1. Pick a Spot

Plants need some sunlight to grow. So find a sunny spot.

2. Decide What to Grow

You might choose flowers or vegetables. Buy seeds for each kind of plant you choose.

3. Plant the Seeds

Read and follow the directions on the seed package. They explain how deep and far apart to plant the seeds.

4. Water Your Garden

Water your garden every day or every other day to keep the soil moist.

5. Watch Your Garden Grow

Soon you will see little sprouts popping up through the soil. Enjoy your growing garden!

Think about a task that you have completed. Write a text that explains how to do this task. Use this space to plan your writing. Write your text on your own sheet of paper.

_____

_____

Multiple-Meaning Words

Skill Overview

Some words have more than one meaning. Context clues are important when a word has more than one meaning. The context clues help you know which meaning to use.

Read the sentences below. In the first sentence, the word <u>jam</u> means "a fruit spread." In the second sentence, <u>jam</u> means "to press" or "to squeeze."

I took the jar of <u>jam</u> from the full refrigerator.

I had to <u>jam</u> it back in after I finished making my sandwich.

Read these sentences. Use context clues to figure out the meaning of the word <u>glasses</u> as it is used in each sentence.

Gina set the table with plates and <u>glasses</u>.

Mom put on her <u>glasses</u> to read the recipe.

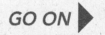
GO ON

Name _____ Date _____

Apply to Text

Read the story. Then answer the questions.

A Little Night Music

1   Last week, my brother had a baseball game in Savannah. It was an important game, so my whole family went to see him play.

2   The game was very close. Every time my brother's team scored a run, the other team would score, too. We thought the game would likely end in a tie.

3   Finally, it was my brother's turn. The pitcher threw the ball. My brother swung the bat. CRACK! The ball sailed into the air. We all cheered as my brother tagged each base. His team, the Lions, won the game.

4   After the game, we bought some sandwiches and drinks for a picnic. Then we walked to the Savannah River. Dad said we could have our picnic while we waited for the evening. Then we would see a show!

5   We joined many other people in downtown Savannah. Everyone crowded around. I didn't know what they were waiting for. Then, suddenly, I heard music!

6   Savannah is home to the largest music
     arts event in Georgia. We heard all
     different kinds of instruments that night.
     My favorite was the bass, which looks just
     like a regular guitar. It was played by a
     man wearing a colorful tie.

7   I liked the sound of all the music. I bobbed
     my head up and down in time with the
     songs. "This is great!" I said. "Thank you for
     bringing us here!" It was a really great day!

1   What is the meaning of <u>tie</u> in the sentence?

> We thought the game would likely end in a <u>tie</u>.

   A a necktie

   B an even score

   C to fasten together

   D to make a knot or a bow

> **Look Closely**
>
> Reread Paragraph 2. Look for context clues that help you figure out which meaning for the word <u>tie</u> is used in the paragraph.

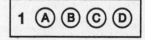

Name _____ Date _____

2 What is the meaning of <u>bat</u> in the sentence?

My brother swung the <u>bat</u>.

A a flying mammal

B to blink very quickly

C to hit back and forth

D a wooden stick or club

3 What is the meaning of <u>bass</u> in the sentence?

My favorite was the <u>bass</u>, which looks just like a
regular guitar.

A a man with a low voice

B a string instrument

C a large fish

D the low part of the music

4 What is the meaning of <u>tie</u> in the sentence?

It was played by a man wearing a colorful <u>tie</u>.

A a necktie

B an even score

C to fasten together

D to make a knot or a bow

2 Ⓐ Ⓑ Ⓒ Ⓓ
3 Ⓐ Ⓑ Ⓒ Ⓓ
4 Ⓐ Ⓑ Ⓒ Ⓓ

STOP

Name _____ Date _____

Writing and Research

Overview

Sometimes you will be asked to read two texts and then use both texts to answer a question. You will write a paragraph. When you write, use facts and details from the texts to support your answer.

Step 1: Plan Your Writing

Decide what you will write about. You might use a chart or web to help organize your ideas.

Step 2: Write a First Draft

Use your ideas to write a first draft. First, introduce the topic and texts. Then state your main ideas. Include facts and details from the two texts. Make sure your ideas are organized in a way that makes sense. Include an ending that sums up your ideas.

Step 3: Revise Your Writing

When you revise, you make changes. You might add or take out words. You might add details. You might move sentences to group ideas together.

Step 4: Edit Your Writing

Check your writing for errors in spelling or grammar. When you **edit,** you correct errors.

Step 5: Write a Final Draft

Write your final draft. As you write, make sure to include all your changes. Make sure your conclusion sums up your ideas. Use your best handwriting.

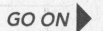

GO ON ▶

Writing Practice

Read the two texts that follow. Take notes on each one. After you read, follow the directions to write a paragraph about what you have read.

Using Clues to Learn about the Past

Do you like solving mysteries? If so, you may want to become an archaeologist when you grow up.

Archaeologists dig up and study very old objects. These objects are called artifacts. Archaeologists study artifacts to learn how people lived a long time ago. They can learn what kinds of tools people used. They can learn what kinds of houses people lived in. They can even describe what an ancient village might have looked like.

Archaeologists have to dig carefully. They do not want to break any buried objects. When they find artifacts, they use small brushes to remove the dirt. They take the artifacts to a lab to clean them. Then they can examine the artifacts closely and figure out how people used them long ago.

What do archaeologists learn from studying artifacts?

_____

_____

Kolomoki Mounds State Park

Kolomoki Mounds State Historic Park in Georgia is a great place to visit. It is not just a park. It is also an important archaeological site. It is the oldest and largest Woodland Indian site in the southeastern United States.

There are seven mounds in the park. The largest is called the Temple Mound. It is 56 feet tall. Archaeologists believe the Kolomoki people used one of the mounds as a calendar. By watching where the sun rose over the mound, the ancient people could tell the month of the year.

The park has a museum. It is built around one of the mounds. You can walk through the museum and see objects where ancient people left them.

The next time you want to learn about the past, take a trip to Kolomoki Mounds State Historic Park. Discover more clues about how people lived long ago.

What is special about Kolomoki Mounds State Historic Park?

_____

_____

GO ON ▶

Think about the two texts you have read. Write a paragraph to explain what archaeologists can teach us about how people lived long ago. Use facts and details from both texts in your writing.

Use this space to plan your writing. Write your paragraph on your own sheet of paper.

_____

_____

_____

_____

_____

STOP

Read Together

Compare and Contrast

How to Analyze the Text

The story *Yeh-Shen* tells about Yeh-Shen; her stepmother, Jin; and her stepsister, Jun-li. The story is like the European story of Cinderella in some important ways. It is different from Cinderella in some important ways, too. You can tell how the stories are alike and different by using **compare** and **contrast**.

When you **compare** stories, you tell how they are alike. When you **contrast** them, you tell how they are different. Knowing how the two stories are alike and different can help the reader better understand both the stories.

This diagram compares and contrasts the stories of Cinderella and Yeh-Shen.

Yeh-Shen
fish bones grant wishes, silk slippers, marries a king

Both
lose one slipper

Cinderella
fairy godmother grants wishes, glass slippers, marries a prince

The phrases in the left circle are true of Yeh-Shen but not of Cinderella. The phrases in the right circle are true of Cinderella but not of Yeh-Shen. The phrase in the middle is true of both stories.

GO ON ▶

Apply to Text

Read the story. Then answer the questions.

Oochigeaska: A Cinderella Story of the Mik'maq Indians

1   In a village at the edge of a lake lived a great hunter. He was invisible to everyone except his sister. It was said that he would marry any other woman that could see his sled strap, his bow string, and him.

2   Many young women came to visit the invisible hunter. When the sister would ask what the sled strap and bow string were made of, though, no one ever gave the right answer.

3   Nearby there lived a man with three daughters. The older daughters made fun of the youngest one. They made her do all the work. They called her Oochigeaska, or "burnt-skin girl," because her face was dark from working under the hot sun. Oochigeaska never complained or teased them back.

4   One day, Oochigeaska dressed in her rags and leggings of birch bark and went to the wigwam of the invisible hunter.

5   First, Oochigeaska met the invisible hunter's sister. She took Oochigeaska down to the lake where her brother was. "Do you see him?" she asked.

6   "I do!" Oochigeaska exclaimed.

Look Closely

How is this part of the story like the story of Cinderella? How is it different?

Name _____ Date _____

7   "What is his sled strap made of?" the
    sister asked. "And his bow string?"

8   "It is the rainbow," said Oochigeaska.
    "And his bow string is made of stars."

9   She took Oochigeaska to her brother.
    Soon the girl's hair grew long, and her eyes
    twinkled like stars.

10 So the invisible hunter married
    Oochigeaska. And she sat in the wife's seat
    in his wigwam for all the rest of her days.

1   **Complete the chart with TWO details that
    show how Oochigeaska and Cinderella are alike.**

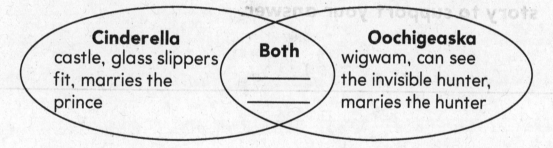

Cinderella
castle, glass slippers
fit, marries the
prince

Both
_____
_____

Oochigeaska
wigwam, can see
the invisible hunter,
marries the hunter

**Explain why these details accurately complete
the chart.**

_____

_____

_____

GO ON ▶

Name _____ Date _____

2 **How is the invisible hunter like the prince in Cinderella? Give ONE detail from the story to support your answer.**

_____

_____

_____

3 **What is true of the Oochigeaska story, but not of the Cinderella story? Give ONE detail from the story to support your answer.**

_____

_____

_____

STOP 🛑

Antonyms

Skill Overview

Think about the story *Two of Everything*. In the story, the author tells how the Haktaks got their gold coins.

"The Haktaks worked late into the night, filling and emptying the pot until the floor was covered with coins."

If you did not know the meaning of <u>emptying</u>, the word <u>filling</u> could help you. The word <u>emptying</u> means the opposite of <u>filling</u>.

This kind of context clue is an antonym. An **antonym** is a word whose meaning is the opposite of the meaning of the unknown word.

Read the examples below. Can you find the antonym for each underlined word?

Example Sentences
The Haktaks were poor at the beginning of the story and <u>wealthy</u> at the end of the story.
Mr. Haktak would begin working at <u>dawn</u> and come home in the evening.
Mrs. Haktak was angry when there were two Mrs. Haktaks. She became <u>calm</u> when the new Mrs. Haktak had her own Mr. Haktak!

GO ON

Apply to Text

Read the story. Then answer the questions.

Making Tracks

1   When you walk on soft dirt or firm sand, look behind you. What are those marks on the ground? Those are your tracks. They are footprints, or the marks your feet leave behind.

2   Animals leave tracks, too. When they walk in mud, sand, or snow, their feet leave marks. Every kind of animal leaves a different kind of track.

3   Cats and dogs leave similar tracks. But if you look closely, you can see how they are different. Cat tracks are rounder than dog tracks. Dog tracks usually have marks from the dog's claws. Cats keep their claws in, so you can't see any claw marks in their tracks.

4   Many bird tracks have three toe marks in front and one toe mark in back. Most bird tracks are narrow, but a duck's tracks are wide. They show the webbed part between the duck's toes.

5   Tracks can tell you what an animal was doing. If a dog was walking, the tracks are close together. If a dog was running, the tracks are far apart.

6   Tracks can tell you the size of an animal. A large, heavy animal will leave deep

tracks in the soft earth. A small, light animal will leave shallow tracks. For example, a huge bear leaves large, deep tracks. But a tiny mouse leaves small, shallow ones.

7   The number of toes you see also tells you about the animal. Deer leave tracks with two toes. The front legs of squirrels and chipmunks leave four-toed tracks. But their back legs leave five-toed tracks.

8   The next time you go for a walk in the woods or on the beach, look carefully at the ground. You might be able to tell what animals walked there before you.

1 In the sentence, which word means the opposite of the word <u>firm</u>?

> When you walk on soft dirt or <u>firm</u> sand, look behind you.

A behind

B dirt

C soft

D walk

Look Closely

Reread Paragraph 1. Look for words that mean the opposite of <u>firm</u>. Remember that an antonym is a word that has an opposite, or very different, meaning.

1 Ⓐ Ⓑ Ⓒ Ⓓ

GO ON ▶

2 Which word from Paragraph 3 is an antonym for the word <u>similar</u>?

   A closely

   B different

   C rounder

   D usually

> **Look Closely**
>
> Reread Paragraph 3. An antonym may appear in the sentence before or after the unknown word.

3 In the sentence, which word means the opposite of the word <u>narrow</u>?

> Most bird tracks are <u>narrow</u>, but a duck's tracks are wide.

   A bird

   B most

   C tracks

   D wide

4 Which word from the passage is an antonym for the word <u>close</u>?

   A far

   B tell

   C together

   D tracks

5 Which word from the passage is an antonym for the word <u>shallow</u>?

   A deep

   B earth

   C heavy

   D large

2 Ⓐ Ⓑ Ⓒ Ⓓ
3 Ⓐ Ⓑ Ⓒ Ⓓ
4 Ⓐ Ⓑ Ⓒ Ⓓ
5 Ⓐ Ⓑ Ⓒ Ⓓ

STOP

Writing Opinions

Overview

When you write an **opinion,** you tell what you think about a topic. You give reasons to support your opinion.

Step 1: Plan Your Writing

Make a list of topics or ideas. Circle the one you want to write about. You might use a chart or web to help you organize your thoughts.

Step 2: Write a First Draft

Use your ideas to write a first draft. First, write a main sentence that tells your opinion. Then write sentences that support your opinion. Write a conclusion that restates your opinion.

Step 3: Revise Your Writing

When you **revise,** you make changes. You might add or take out words. You might add details. You might put reasons in a better order. Maybe you need to add linking words such as <u>because</u> or <u>also</u>. Linking words connect your opinion with your reasons.

Step 4: Edit Your Writing

Check your writing for errors in spelling or grammar. When you **edit,** you correct errors.

Step 5: Write a Final Draft

Write your final draft. As you write, make sure to include all of your changes. Make sure you have a conclusion. Use your best handwriting.

GO ON ▶

Name _____ Date _____

Writing Practice

Read the text. Then follow the directions.

Old Inventions

We live very differently today than people did 100 years ago. However, some of the inventions from many years ago are still important parts of our lives.

The Wright Brothers invented the airplane in 1903. The first flight lasted for only 12 seconds. Back then no one could have known how popular airplanes would become. Today, millions of people fly on airplanes each year.

The television was invented in the 1920s. In the early years, there were only a few channels. Shows were in black and white. Televisions today receive hundreds of channels. But just like long ago, families like to sit together to enjoy a favorite program.

Technology keeps changing. Inventors continue to come up with new products and new ways of doing things. Imagine what inventions will be made 100 years from now!

Think of another important invention. Plan and write an opinion paragraph to tell why you think the invention is important. Write your paragraph on your own sheet of paper.

STOP

Reading Practice Test

Part 1

Read the story. Then answer the questions.

Save the Cat!

1   A cat named Molly lived in a store in New York City. You may think it's strange to have a cat in a store, but Molly was a popular cat. Many people shopped at the store each day. These people knew Molly. They all liked to see her and pet her.

2   One day, Molly wasn't there. Everyone wondered where she was. The store seemed like an empty place without her.

3   The people in the store were worried about Molly, so they started looking for her. Soon, they began hearing noises. They could hear a cat crying. The cries were coming from behind the wall. Other people walking outside the store heard the cries, too. Everyone knew it was Molly!

4   The people saw a small opening between the wall of the store and the building next door. Molly had gone into the opening. The people could hear Molly, but they could not see her. They called to Molly. They wanted her to come out. Molly cried back, but she didn't come. She couldn't get out by herself. Molly was trapped between the walls!

GO ON ▶

5   Everyone knew Molly needed their help. They called animal workers to rescue Molly. The workers wanted to free Molly. They tried many different things to get Molly to come out.

6   The animal workers held a basket of kittens near the opening. They hoped that Molly would hear the kittens and come out to care for them, but Molly didn't come.

7   Next the workers played sounds of birds chirping by the opening. They hoped Molly would hear the sounds and come to see if the birds were really there. Molly still didn't come. Then they put fresh fish by the opening. They hoped Molly would smell the fish and come out to eat. But Molly still didn't come.

8   Reporters wrote about Molly in the newspapers. They talked about Molly on the TV news. People all over the world heard about Molly. Everyone wanted her to be safe.

9   Two weeks passed. Molly was still lost between the walls of the building. Finally, workers used special tools to carefully cut new holes in the wall. They put cameras in the holes to see if they could see Molly. They could see her! She was okay! After making a few more holes, the workers finally got Molly out.

10   Everyone cheered when they heard Molly was safe. They were happy to see Molly, and Molly was happy to see them. Everyone came to the store now to visit the famous cat. Molly purred and purred. She loved seeing all the people, and she never went near the hole in the wall again.

1 **What is the MAIN problem in the story?**

    A Molly keeps crying.

    B Molly doesn't like fish.

    C Molly is trapped between the walls.

    D Molly is not very friendly around people.

2 **Which word in Paragraph 5 helps the reader know what the word <u>rescue</u> means?**

    A called

    B help

    C tried

    D things

3 **Why couldn't people see Molly?**

    A Molly was lost in New York City.

    B The opening in the wall was too small.

    C Molly lived in a store.

    D The people weren't looking hard enough.

GO ON ▶

4 Look at the flow chart.

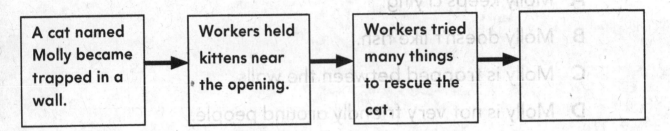

| A cat named Molly became trapped in a wall. | → | Workers held kittens near the opening. | → | Workers tried many things to rescue the cat. | → | |

Which event belongs in the empty box?

A People stopped going to the store every day.

B Workers couldn't think of a way to save the cat.

C People decided to let the cat live in the wall.

D Workers cut holes in the wall to get Molly out.

5 What can the reader tell about Molly at the end of the story?

A Molly is very happy to be back in the store.

B Molly is ready to have another adventure.

C Molly wishes she had stayed in the wall.

D Molly wants to chase all the people away.

Read the passage. Then answer the questions.

Working with Animals

1   Do you love animals? If so, you might adopt a pet
to join your family. Some people love animals so much
that they work with them all day long. These people are
called animal workers. There are many kinds of animal
workers.

When Animals Get Sick

2   Veterinarians, or vets, are doctors for animals. Vets
figure out what illness an animal has. Then they figure
out a way to treat that illness. Some vets only care for
cats, dogs, and birds. Other vets care for livestock, such
as horses, cows, sheep, and pigs. There are even vets for
zoo animals, like zebras and monkeys. Vets go to school
for many years to learn their jobs.

When Animals Need Care

3   Kennel workers take care of pets while their owners are
away. A kennel is a shelter for cats and dogs. It's like a
hotel for pets. Pet owners bring their pets to the kennel.
The kennel workers there make sure the pets are fed and
cared for. Kennel workers might have many pets staying
in the kennel at one time.

GO ON

Name _____ Date _____

4   Pet sitters also care for animals when their owners are away. A pet sitter is like a babysitter for a pet. Most times, the pet sitter goes to the pet's home. Sometimes, the pet goes to stay at the pet sitter's home. Either way, the pet sitter makes sure the pet is safe and happy.

When Animals Are in Danger

5   Animal rescuers help pets that might be hurt or lost. Some rescuers take special classes to learn how to help animals. They can also learn while doing their job. Animal rescuers try all kinds of things to save animals in trouble. They often work with vets to help injured animals, too.

6   There are a lot of people who help take care of our animal friends. Maybe one day you'll decide to be an animal worker, too. There are certainly a lot of ways you can do it.

6 **What are <u>animal workers</u>?**

   A animals that do jobs for people

   B people who take care of animals

   C animals that work on farms

   D people who make animals work

7 **What is the base word of <u>rescuers</u>?**

   A cue

   B escue

   C cures

   D rescue

8 **Which animal workers are described under the heading "When Animals Get Sick"?**

   A animal rescuers

   B kennel workers

   C veterinarians

   D pet sitters

GO ON ▶

Name _____ Date _____

9 Which animal worker would MOST LIKELY come to your house to watch your pet?

  A animal rescuer

  B kennel worker

  C pet sitter

  D veterinarian

10 How are the passages "Working with Animals" and the story "Save the Cat!" alike?

  A They both tell about people who help animals.

  B They both tell what happens to Molly the cat.

  C They both tell fictional stories about animals.

  D They both tell how to adopt a new pet.

Name _____ Date _____

Read the poem. Then answer the questions.

A Day with an Elephant

I'm spending the day with an elephant,

And here are some things that we'll do.

We'll parade up and down

All the streets of our town,

5   And we'll visit our friends at the zoo.

We will eat only popcorn and applesauce.

And maybe some chocolate cake, too!

When you're spending the day with an elephant,

Those are the things that you do.

10   My friend Billy Ray wants to come with us.

So I say, "Billy Ray, that depends.

You can come right along!

But you must sing a song

About kids and their animal friends."

15   Then he laughs and says, "Jake, you're a funny guy!

Sure, I'll make up a song just for you.

You are spending the day with an elephant,

And I really want to come, too!"

GO ON ▶

My friend Lila Jane has a cockatoo.

20   Lila Jane can hear Billy Ray singing loud.

She comes out to the street,

In a dress and bare feet,

With her cockatoo whistling proud.

Lila Jane says, "I want to parade with you!"

25   Her big bird wants to come along, too.

We are spending the day with an elephant.

There is nothing else better to do!

When the sun goes down,

Our fun's at an end.

30   But hip, hip, hooray!

We love spending the day

With our giant, gray elephant friend.

11 Who is the speaker of the poem?

   A Billy Ray

   B Jake

   C Lila Jane

   D an elephant

12 Where does the action of the poem take place?

   A a park

   B a school

   C a circus

   D a town

13 What does Billy Ray do to spend the day with an elephant?

   A He makes up a song.

   B He goes to the zoo alone.

   C He brings chocolate cake.

   D He whistles out loud.

GO ON ▶

Name _____ Date _____

14 **Which words mean the SAME as <u>parade</u> in Line 3 and Line 24?**

   A tiptoe quietly

   B walk carefully

   C march proudly

   D run quickly

15 **What is a <u>cockatoo</u>?**

   A a kind of an elephant

   B a kind of a dress

   C a kind of a song

   D a kind of a bird

16 **Which event happens LAST in the poem?**

   A The cockatoo whistles.

   B The sun goes down.

   C Billy Ray sings for Jake.

   D Lila Jane hears Billy Ray.

17 **How do the kids in the poem feel about spending the day with an elephant?**

   A sad and fearful

   B worried and nervous

   C happy and excited

   D quiet and thoughtful

Read and answer the questions.

18 Which sentence has correct end punctuation?

    A Will you come with me.

    B Do you have a pet hamster!

    C Which pizza tastes the best?

    D Who is going to the party.

19 Which of these is a complete sentence?

    A I forgot my glasses.

    B Brown with red stripes.

    C How I will see them.

    D Walked carefully along.

20 Choose the SUBJECT and the VERB in the sentence.

Marcy brought a bright red ball to the beach.

    A Marcy, to

    B brought, ball

    C Marcy, bright

    D Marcy, brought

GO ON

Read the story. Then answer the questions.

Pete's Play

(1) Pete was nervous. (2) It was the day of the school play. (3) He had a part. (4) What if he messed up? (5) His friend Mike told him not to worry. (6) "Everyone messes up sometimes," Mike said. (7) "The important thing is not to give up." (8) Mike had on a yellow shirt. (9) Suddenly, it was time to start. (10) Pete was so surprized that he forgot about being nervous. (11) He played his part the best he could. (12) He messed up one time, but he kept going.

---

21 **Which word could be added to Sentence 3 to show more detail about Pete's part?**

> He had a part.

A big

B only

C nothing

D school

22 **Which sentence is NOT needed and should be removed from the paragraph?**

A Pete was nervous.

B He had a part.

C Mike had on a yellow shirt.

D Suddenly, it was time to start.

23 **Which sentence BEST fits at the end of the story?**

A Pete felt terrible about it.

B The play was a big success.

C He never wanted to be in the play.

D Everyone went home early.

24 **What is the correct way to write the underlined word in Sentence 10?**

> Pete was so <u>surprized</u> that he forgot about being nervous.

A supprized

B surprised

C supprised

D suprised

STOP

Part 2

Read the instructions. Then answer the questions.

Growing Bean Sprouts

1   Do you know how seeds grow? Usually, seeds are planted deep in the ground. We can't see what they do down there. Here's an easy experiment you can try without soil that will let you see the seeds grow right before your eyes.

2   **What You Need**

- a quart jar with a wide mouth
- a lid for the jar
- a handful of dry beans
- water and soap

What to Do

3   First, wash and dry the jar and the lid with soap and water. Ask an adult to poke 10 holes in the lid.

4   Next, wash the beans in water. Do not use soap on the beans. Put the beans in the jar. Fill the jar with water. Put the lid on the jar. Put the jar of beans in a dark place. Make sure the jar is secure and won't tip over. Leave the jar there for one night.

5   The next day, pour the water out of the jar through the holes in the lid. Shake the jar to get out all the water. Then turn the jar on its side. This will give the beans some room to spread out. Put the jar back in its dark place.

6   Twice a day, rinse the beans and pour out the water. Keep the jar on its side in the dark. Within two days, the shell of each bean will crack a little, and a sprout will appear.

7   This is what happens to seeds when they are in the ground. The first sprouts from a seed become the roots of the plant. Then, as the seed continues to grow, a sprout will become the part of the plant that pushes up through the ground.

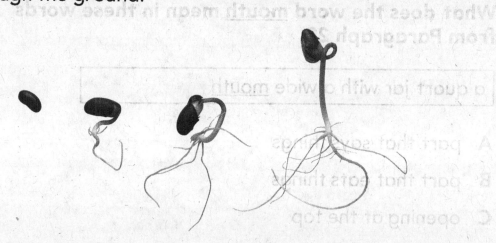

The sprout becomes the roots and stem of a plant.

GO ON ▶

Name _____ Date _____

25 What is this passage mostly about?

    A what bean sprouts are used for

    B the history of bean sprouts

    C where to find bean sprouts

    D how to grow bean sprouts

26 Which of these do you NOT need to grow bean sprouts?

    A soil

    B water

    C a dark place

    D a jar

27 What does the word <u>mouth</u> mean in these words from Paragraph 2?

a quart jar with a wide <u>mouth</u>

    A part that says things

    B part that eats things

    C opening at the top

    D beginning of a river

28 What does the word <u>handful</u> mean in these words from Paragraph 2?

a <u>handful</u> of dry beans

A full of hands

B enough to fill a hand

C having many hands

D beans as big as a hand

29 What should you do AFTER you shake the jar?

A Turn the jar on its side.

B Fill the jar with water.

C Poke holes in the lid.

D Put the beans in the jar.

30 What is the effect of turning the jar on its side?

A This gets all the water out of the jar.

B This keeps the beans from moving around.

C This gives the beans room to spread out.

D This keeps all the water in the jar.

31 What does the picture at the end of the passage show?

A how to put the beans in the jar

B what kind of beans to use

C how a bean grows into a plant

D where to put the jar to grow sprouts

GO ON

Name _____ Date _____

32 Which of these would be the BEST resource to get more information about how seeds grow?

A an encyclopedia

B a dictionary

C a newspaper

D a glossary

Read the story. Then answer the questions.

Under the Old Oak Tree

1   Jen stood on the porch and looked around. She was spending the summer with her family at the old country house where her great-grandmother grew up. Oak trees dotted the field in front of the house. It was beautiful, but the problem was Jen was already tired of oak trees. Her best friend Madison was back home, and Jen was stuck here for the summer with nothing to do.

2   Jen walked to the old toolshed, where her dog Rags was clawing at something in the dirt. What was it? Jen gently pushed Rags aside and started digging with her hands. At last, she uncovered an old box. She tugged at the latch and lifted the top.

3   Inside, Jen found a piece of paper with a drawing of an oak tree. A big X was marked on the ground under the tree. What was the X for? Suddenly, she knew.

4   "It's a treasure map!" she cried. She ran out of the shed and looked around. There were so many oak trees! Which one was on the map? Jen looked at the picture for clues. She saw the letters NB drawn on the tree. Then Jen saw the word *lago* next to the X.

5   Jen ran to the house with the map. She showed it to her dad and asked, "What does *lago* mean?"

GO ON

Name _____ Date _____

6   "I think it's Spanish," Dad said. "Why don't you go next door and see Luz. Maybe she will know."

7   Luz's family had just moved into the house next door, and Jen had only met her once. Jen was shy about talking to Luz, but she really wanted to find the tree. Finally, Jen bravely went over and knocked on their door.

8   When Luz answered, Jen showed her the map. Luz smiled, "I know what *lago* means. Is there a lake around here?"

9   "There is a lake at the end of the field," Jen said. "Come check it out with me!" Jen grabbed a shovel from the shed and led the way to the lake.

10   Luz and Jen searched each tree around the lake. They found the letters NB carved into the seventh tree.

11   "What now?" Luz asked.

12   "Now we dig!" Jen said.

13 Soon, they found another old box. Inside was a picture of a young girl, with the words "Nina Batista, age 8" written on the back.

14 "She looks just like you," Luz said.

15 "That's my great-grandmother!" Jen said. "She grew up here."

16 At the bottom of the box were a small gold ring and a painted hairclip. Jen put the ring on her finger. She gave the hairclip to Luz.

17 "What good is a treasure if you can't share it?" Jen said. "Besides, you helped figure it all out."

18 Jen and Luz walked back to the house. On the way, they made plans for their next adventure. Jen had a feeling that maybe it would not be such a bad summer after all.

33 How does Jen feel at the beginning of the story?

    A happy

    B bored

    C silly

    D worried

GO ON ▶

34 **Which word means the opposite of <u>uncovered</u> in this sentence?**

> At last, she <u>uncovered</u> an old box.

A dug up

B found

C discovered

D hid

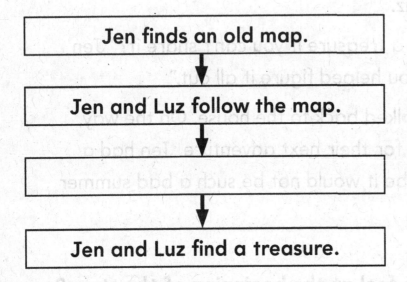

Jen finds an old map.

↓

Jen and Luz follow the map.

↓

↓

Jen and Luz find a treasure.

35 **Read the chart.**

Which event belongs in the empty box?

A Jen gives Luz a painted hairpin.

B Jen and Luz find the tree marked NB.

C Jen digs a hole by the old toolshed.

D Jen takes a picture of her great-grandmother.

Name _____ Date _____

36 What does the picture in the story show?

A the place where Jen finds the map

B the yard behind Luz's new house

C the house where Jen is spending the summer

D the lake where Jen and Luz find the treasure

37 How are Jen and Luz the SAME?

A They both are happy to make a new friend.

B They both know how to speak Spanish.

C They both do not like to have adventures.

D They both want to do nothing all summer.

38 Which of these resources would MOST LIKELY help Jen figure out the meaning of the word lago?

A an Internet search for the word

B a newspaper article in Spanish

C a picture book about lakes

D a storybook about lost treasure

GO ON

Read the letter. Then answer the questions.

Notes from New York

From: OllieTheGreat@xyz.com

To: SuperManSam@abc.com

Date: December 15

Dear Sam,

1   How are you? We are in our new home in New York. I miss you and all our friends at school. I thought I would be unhappy here, but I have made a few new friends. You're still my best friend, though.

2   Things are very different here, but some things are the same. You know that in Georgia I lived on King Street. Well, in New York I also live on King Street! My school is nearby, so I walk now instead of taking a bus. Also, our house in Georgia had a big backyard where Patches could run and play. Here, our apartment is kind of small, and we do not have a yard. There is a nice park only two blocks away, though. Three times a day, we take Patches for a walk there. He seems to like it a lot, even in the winter.

3   Last Saturday, I had my first sled ride. It was more work than I thought. We had to pull the sled all the way up a steep hill. Once we got to the top of the hill, we sat on the sled and hung on tight as we went sailing down

Name _____ Date _____

the slope. It was a lot of fun, but it would have been
more fun if you were there. Mom made me hot chocolate
when I got home. I laughed and told her that if we were
in Georgia, she'd be making me lemonade instead.

4   I hope you can come visit sometime. Write back
soon, okay?

Your pal,

Oliver

39 Who wrote this letter?

A   Sam

B   Oliver

C   Mom

D   Patches

**40 Why does Oliver have to take Patches for walks in
the park?**

A   because it is winter

B   because they live on a hill

C   because they do not have a yard

D   because the park is far away

GO ON ▶

41 **Which happened FIRST in the sled ride?**

   A They sat on the sled.

   B They hung on tight.

   C They sailed down the slope.

   D They pulled the sled up the hill.

42 **According to Oliver, the sled ride would have been better if**

   A the weather had been warmer.

   B Sam had been there.

   C the hill had been less steep.

   D Mom had served lemonade.

43 **How does Oliver feel about his new home?**

   A He likes it better than his old home.

   B He likes it, but he misses his best friend.

   C He hates it, and he wants to move back.

   D He loves it, and he never wants to leave.

Name _____ Date _____

Read and answer the questions.

44 **Which word is the VERB in this sentence?**

> Jayla painted flowers on her bedroom wall.

- A painted
- B flowers
- C bedroom
- D wall

45 **Which sentence uses capital letters correctly?**

- A I live in the blue house on fourth Street.
- B Miss jackson teaches us art on Tuesdays.
- C We are driving from Atlanta to Savannah.
- D My Sandwich has the crusts cut off.

46 **What is the correct way to write the underlined word?**

> My favorite animals at the zoo are the <u>monkey</u>.

- A monkies
- B monkeyes
- C monkeys
- D monkeyys

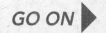
GO ON

Name _____ Date _____

47 **What is the correct way to write the underlined word?**

> Jeremiah is <u>short</u> than his sister.

A shorter

B shortest

C more short

D most short

48 **Which sentence uses pronouns correctly?**

A Me love to read books about cowboys.

B Him went to the store to buy new shoes.

C Them are having a swimming party.

D She wants to be a doctor one day.

49 **Which resource is the BEST to use to find out about something that happened yesterday?**

A an encyclopedia

B a dictionary

C a newspaper

D a picture book

50 What can you tell about the girl in the picture?

A   She does not like to make drawings.

B   She is proud of the drawing she made.

C   She is afraid to show the picture she drew.

D   She thinks drawing is a silly thing to do.

STOP

Writing to Narrate

Performance Task

Read the text. Then follow the directions.

Birthday Surprise!

My grandparents used to live around the corner from our house. Then, they moved to Arizona, more than 1,800 miles away! I was sad because I missed them so much.

Last weekend was my eighth birthday. Mom and Dad woke me up early and hurried me to the car. Mom said we were going somewhere important. I asked where, but Mom wouldn't explain.

Soon I could see we were at the airport. We drove past a sign that said "Arriving Flights." Dad stopped the car near the curb, and I looked out the window. There were my grandparents!

"Surprise, Hollis! Happy birthday!" they shouted. Seeing them was the best birthday present ever.

Plan and write a story about a time you were surprised or you surprised someone else. Include details. Write your story on your own sheet of paper.

STOP

Writing to Inform

Performance Task

Read the text. Then follow the directions.

Packing for the Beach

Suppose you are going on a beach vacation. You will have to pack your suitcase with everything that you will need.

First, count how many days you will be gone. Then, lay out enough shirts, shorts, and other clothes for your trip. Next, pack personal care items. Include a toothbrush, toothpaste, and shampoo.

Then think about what you will need at the beach. You will need a bathing suit. You might want to pack goggles, flip-flops, and beach toys. Don't forget the sunblock.

Now everything is organized and zipped into your suitcase. You are ready to have a great time at the beach!

Think of a place you would like to go on vacation. Plan and write a paragraph to tell what you would need to pack. Include details. Write your paragraph on your own sheet of paper.

STOP

Writing Opinions

Performance Task

Read the text. Then follow the directions.

Thanksgiving on Stage

The second grade class voted for their favorite holiday. Thanksgiving won. The class decided to put on a play to celebrate this special holiday.

Miss Rojas explained that a play needs actors and actresses. She said, "Everyone will get a part. We also need students to write the play and build sets."

Ben agreed and said, "I can't wait for our families to see our play. This will be the very best way to start our Thanksgiving celebrations."

Write an opinion paragraph to tell which holiday is your favorite. Give reasons to support your opinion.

Use this space to plan your writing. Write your opinion paragraph on your own sheet of paper.

_____

_____

STOP

Name _____ Date _____

Writing and Research

Performance Task

Read the two texts that follow. Take notes on each one. After you read, follow the directions to write a paragraph about what you have read.

Safe Surfing

The Internet is an amazing tool. However, it also can be dangerous. Follow these rules to be safe.

Make sure you have permission to go online. Tell your parents what you are searching for or what game you are playing. They can make sure the Web sites are safe.

A Web site may look like it has great information. But ask an adult to help you make sure the Web site gives facts and not opinions. If you are asked questions online, never give your name, address, or other personal information.

Use the Internet safely. Then you can do your homework, keep in touch with friends, and have fun.

What are some ways you can safely use the Internet?

_____

_____

Hello Telephone!

Alexander Graham Bell invented the telephone in 1876. Soon the telephone would become an important part of people's lives.

The first telephones were large and bulky. They didn't have ringers. Instead, the caller tapped the phone with a hammer. This let the other person know a call was coming in.

Today, many people have cell phones. They are small and easy to carry. People can use them to make calls almost anywhere. Cell phones are used for more than just calling. Many of today's cell phones can be used to text, get to the Internet, listen to music, and take pictures.

Alexander Graham Bell would be surprised to see his invention today. Who knows what phones will be like in the future!

How has the telephone changed over time?

_____

_____

STOP

Think about the two texts you have read. Write a paragraph to explain how the Internet and telephones help people. Use facts and details from both texts in your writing.

Use this space to plan your writing. Write your paragraph on your own sheet of paper.

STOP

Reading/Writing Practice Test

Read the passage. Then answer the questions.

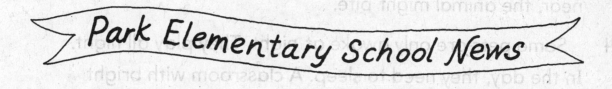

Park Elementary School News

No Pets in the Classroom

by Fran Woods,
parent of two Park Elementary School students

1   Many classrooms have pets.
What kinds of pets have you seen in
classrooms? Hamsters, mice, guinea
pigs, rabbits, fish, and turtles can
be found in classrooms. However, I
believe a classroom is no place for
pets. There are many reasons for this.

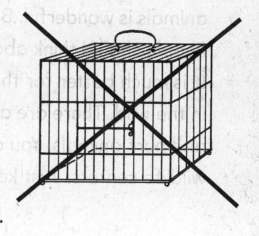

2   Some pets need a lot of care. But classroom pets may
be left alone on weekends or school holidays. Even if
food is left for the pets, they do not get the care they
need. What if the animals needed vet care? If no one
is checking on the animals, then no one will know if the
animals are sick.

GO ON ▶

3   Some pets need quiet homes. Classrooms can get noisy. Sometimes there is a lot of movement in a classroom. These things may scare the animal. Then the animal may feel a need to protect itself. If a child came near, the animal might bite.

4   Some pets are only awake at night. They play all night. In the day, they need to sleep. A classroom with bright lights and loud sounds is not the best place for this kind of pet.

5   Many teachers bring pets in the classroom to help children learn more about animals. Learning about animals is wonderful. But an animal is a living thing. People should think about what is best for the animal. It is much better for the animals if people watch them in the wild. There are also wildlife centers that help sick and hurt animals. You can learn about many animals at wildlife centers. Just keep animals out of the classroom!

1 Complete the web with ONE detail from the passage.

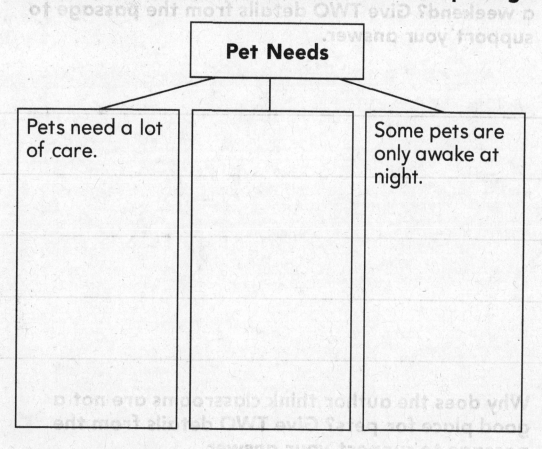

Pet Needs

| Pets need a lot of care. | | Some pets are only awake at night. |

Explain why this detail completes the web. Use evidence from the text.

_____

_____

_____

_____

_____

_____

GO ON ▶

2 What might happen if a classroom pet got sick on a weekend? Give TWO details from the passage to support your answer.

_____

_____

_____

_____

3 Why does the author think classrooms are not a good place for pets? Give TWO details from the passage to support your answer.

_____

_____

_____

_____

4 **What is the MAIN purpose of this passage? Use evidence from the text to support your answer.**

_____

_____

_____

_____

_____

STOP

Name

Date

Unit 4
PRACTICE 154

Common Core
Reading/Writing

4. What is the MAIN purpose of this passage? Use evidence from the text to support your answer.

Reading/Writing Practice Test

Read the story. Then answer the questions.

Looking for a Good One

1   "I found a good one!" yelled Todd. He held up a large seashell as Mom, Dad, and Todd's twin brother Jesse hurried over to see.

2   Todd and Jesse liked to collect shells. They kept their collection on a shelf in their bedroom. The shells reminded the boys of their trips to the beach. It was the end of their weekend at Parksville Beach, and Todd and Jesse wanted to get a few more shells before it was time to leave.

3   "Wow, it isn't even broken!" Jesse said when he saw the shell up close. "I wish I had found it. All the shells I find are in pieces."

4   Todd turned the shell over in his hands. It felt smooth and round. The outside of the shell was white, but the inside was purple and pink. Todd dropped the shell carefully into a bucket. "This will look really good on the shelf," he said. He turned and walked along the water's edge, looking for more shells.

5   Jesse frowned as he watched his brother walk away.

6   Jesse kicked the sand. Then he looked down. A rounded shell was sticking up out of the sand. "I found a good one!" he yelled.

7   "Good job!" Todd called out.

8   But as Jesse pulled the shell out of the sand, he saw that one end was broken. He tossed the shell back onto the beach. "Todd gets all the luck," he sighed.

9   "You'll find one," Mom said. "Keep trying."

10   "I found a good one!" Todd yelled. He held up another unbroken shell that had been under the water.

11   "I'm going to look where nobody else has looked," Jesse said. He walked away from the water's edge. When he got to a patch of tall grass, something caught his eye. He knelt down to look more closely.

12   "Hey!" Jesse called. "I found a good one!"

13   "What is it?" Mom asked. The rest of the family hurried to his side.

14   "It's a big huge shell!" Jesse exclaimed. The shell was brown and bumpy, and it was bigger than any of the shells Todd had found. "I'm going to take it home," Jesse said. But just as he reached out to grab the shell, it moved!

15   Jesse jumped back as the "shell" trotted off a few feet and stopped. "What in the world is that?" he wanted to know.

16   "It's a crab," Mom explained. "Looks like you won't be adding that shell to your collection. That shell is already in use!"

17   Todd held his nose and said, "I only want shells that nobody lives in!"

18   "I have a great idea!" said Mom. She went to the car and brought back some drawing paper and some crayons. "Since you can't take this shell home," she suggested, "you can draw pictures of it!"

19   That was exactly what the boys did. When they got home, they put the new shells Todd had found on their shelf. They put the drawings of the in-use shell on the shelf, too. The pictures reminded them of the funny thing that happened when they were collecting shells at Parksville Beach. And each picture had a label to help them remember, too:

20   "WE FOUND A GOOD ONE!" the labels said.

GO ON ▶

1 **What are Jesse's feelings at the beginning of the story?.What are Todd's feelings? Give TWO details from the story to support your answer.**

_____

_____

_____

_____

_____

2 **How do Todd and Jesse get along? Give TWO details from the story to support your answer.**

_____

_____

_____

_____

_____

_____

3 Jesse and Todd say "I found a good one!" many times during the story. Why does the author have the characters say this line so many times? Use evidence from the text to support your answer.

_____

_____

_____

_____

_____

4 Complete the story map with THREE details from the story.

Characters	Setting
Todd, Jesse, Mom	the beach

Plot

Beginning

Middle

End

STOP

Reading/Writing Practice Test

Read the instructions. Then answer the questions.

How to Play Hopscotch

Hopscotch is a fun game that can be played indoors or outdoors. Find a place where it is safe for kids to play and you can draw on the ground with chalk. Then follow these steps.

Here is what you need:

colored chalk so you can use fun colors

a marker such as a stone, button, or beanbag

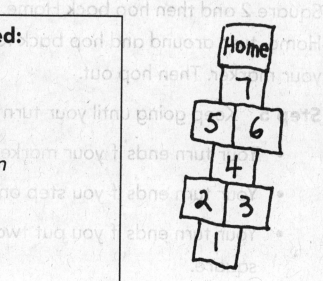

Hopscotch pattern

Here is what you do:

Step 1   Draw a hopscotch pattern on the ground. Use different colors if you want to. Write a number in each square. Write "Home" in the last square.

GO ON ▶

Step 2   When people play hopscotch, they hop on one foot first and then on two feet. Practice hopping on one foot. Can you do that?

Step 3   Now you are ready to play. Toss a marker into Square 1. That is where you start hopping. Hop from Square 1 to Home. You must hop on each square. When you land on Home, turn around and hop back to Square 1. Pick up your marker. Then hop out.

Step 4   Then toss your marker into Square 2. Start in Square 2 and then hop back Home. When you land on Home, turn around and hop back to Square 2. Pick up your marker. Then hop out.

Step 5   Keep going until your turn ends.

- Your turn ends if your marker lands in the wrong square.

- Your turn ends if you step on a line.

- Your turn ends if you put two feet down in a single square.

- Your turn ends if you don't hop in the right squares.

Step 6   The first player to hop the pattern putting the marker in each square wins the game.

1 **How does the picture of the hopscotch pattern help you understand the instructions? Use evidence from the text to support your answer.**

_____

_____

_____

_____

2 **What do you have to do BEFORE you start playing hopscotch? Use evidence from the text to support your answer.**

_____

_____

_____

GO ON ▶

3 **What is Step 5 mainly about? Use evidence from the text to support your answer.**

_____

_____

_____

_____

4   **Think about the order of steps in the instructions.**

   Complete the timeline with TWO details from the instructions.

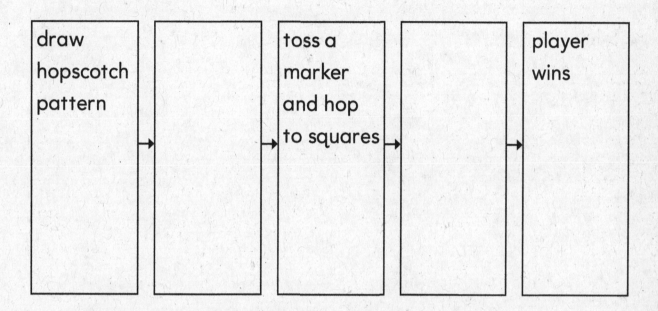

| draw hopscotch pattern | | toss a marker and hop to squares | | player wins |

   Explain why these details accurately complete the timeline. Use evidence from the text.

_____

_____

_____

_____

STOP

Reading/Writing Practice Test

Read the play. Then answer the questions.

Ding-Dong, I Was Writing a Song

Characters:

CHAD (eight-year-old musician)

EMMA

LI

RYAN

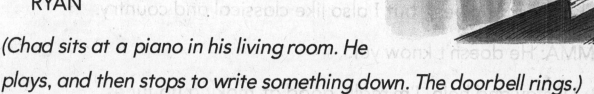

(Chad sits at a piano in his living room. He plays, and then stops to write something down. The doorbell rings.)

CHAD: Every time I sit down to work, someone comes to the door. *(Ding-dong.)* All right, all right, hold your horses, I'm coming.

(Chad gets up and opens the door to let Emma in. Emma is holding a small cookie box.)

EMMA: Hi, Chad. My mom and I made some cookies and we thought you might like some. What are you doing?

CHAD: *(Sits back down at the piano.)* I'm writing a song.

EMMA: Ooh, I *love* songs! What kind of song is it going to be? I like country music, but I like rap and classical, too.

CHAD: Well, I'm not really sure what kind of song it is. Here's what I have so far.

GO ON ▶

I was sitting in the sun one day

I felt I had a lot to say

EMMA: Hey, I like that! *Day* and *say* rhyme. If you want any help, let me know—I am good at rhyming words! (*Ding-dong.*)

(*Emma goes to the door and lets Li in. Li is holding a small kite.*)

LI: Hi, guys! Want to help me fly this kite?

EMMA: Not right now, thanks. You see, Chad is writing a song and I'm trying to help.

LI: Writing a song? That sounds like fun! What kind of a song is it? I like rap music best, but I also like classical and country.

EMMA: He doesn't know yet.

LI: I'll stay and help. I'm really good at making up tunes.

CHAD: I'll think about it.

I was sitting in my room one day

I felt I had a lot to say

A friend or two came to the door…

(*Ding-dong.*)

CHAD: (*Frowns.*) The doorbell is driving me crazy.

EMMA: (*Goes to the door and lets Ryan in.*) Hi, Ryan. Chad is writing a song.

RYAN: What kind of song is it? I like classical music best, but I also like rap and country.

LI: He doesn't know yet.

RYAN: Hey, maybe I can help. I'm good at keeping the beat.

LI: I'm good at making up tunes!

EMMA: I'm good at rhyming words!

CHAD: (*Starting to smile.*) Hey, everyone. I think I have an idea.

(*Singing.*)

Ding-dong,

I was writing a song.

Ding-dong,

I won't be long.

Ding-dong,

You can't go wrong

When you sing along

With this song.

Ding-dong.

ALL: (*Singing together.*)

Ding-dong,

You can't go wrong

When you sing along

With this song.

Ding-dong.

GO ON ▶

1 What can you tell about Chad by looking at the picture on page 163?

_____

_____

_____

_____

2 How does Emma feel about music? Give details from the play to support your answer.

_____

_____

_____

_____

3 **Think about the order of events in the play.
Complete the timeline with ONE detail from the play.**

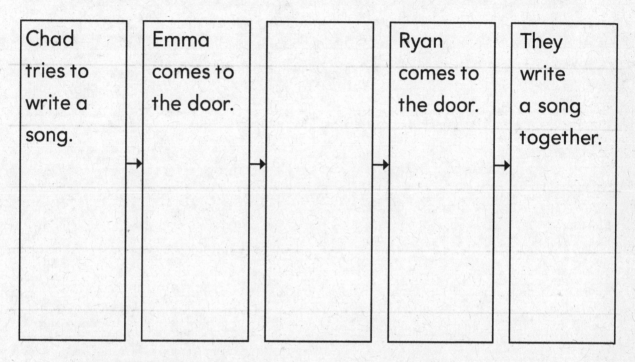

| Chad tries to write a song. | Emma comes to the door. | | Ryan comes to the door. | They write a song together. |

Explain why this detail accurately completes the timeline. Use evidence from the text.

_____

_____

_____

_____

_____

GO ON ▶

4 **Why does Chad repeat certain words in his song? Give TWO details from the play to support your answer.**

_____

_____

_____

_____

STOP

Reading/Writing Practice Test

Read the passage. Then answer the questions.

Spoonbridge and Cherry

1   Let's say that you are walking in a fancy garden. All of a sudden, you see a huge spoon with a cherry on top. The spoon is so big! In fact, it makes a bridge over some water. Would that surprise you? Would that make you laugh?

2   *Spoonbridge and Cherry* is part of the Walker Art Center in Minneapolis, Minnesota. It is a kind of art called a sculpture. It is different from a piece of art like a photo or a painting. Those are flat. A sculpture can be seen from many sides.

3   *Spoonbridge and Cherry* is one big sculpture. The spoon is 52 feet long. That is much longer than a school bus. It is 29 feet high. That is about three stories of a building. The spoon and the cherry together weigh 7,000 pounds.

4   A husband-and-wife team came up with the idea for *Spoonbridge and Cherry*. The husband thought of the spoon as a bridge. His wife thought of the cherry. She thought it would be fun and playful in the middle of a fancy garden.

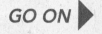
GO ON

5   The two artists work together on many large pieces.
The works of art often look like things we see every day,
but in super size. People seem to enjoy these huge works
of art. The sculptures can be seen in many places around
the world.

Name	When It Was Made	How High It Is
Clothespin	1976	45 feet
Flashlight	1981	39 feet
Saw, Sawing	1996	51 feet
Lion's Tail	1999	19 feet

**1 What is the meaning of the word <u>sculpture</u>? Use
evidence from the text to support your answer.**

_____

_____

_____

_____

Name _____ Date _____

2 What is Paragraph 3 mainly about? Use evidence from the text to support your answer.

_____

_____

_____

_____

GO ON ▶

Read the passage. Then answer the questions.

Grandma Moses

1   Imagine never taking an art lesson but becoming a famous painter. That's what happened to a tiny gray-haired grandmother. Her name was Anna Mary Robertson Moses. People called her Grandma Moses.

2   On September 7, 1860, Anna Mary Robertson was born in upstate New York. She added "Moses" to her name when she married. She and her husband lived in Virginia. They raised their children on a farm. After her husband died in 1927, Moses moved back to New York.

3   Grandma Moses liked to make pictures. First, Grandma Moses loved to sew pictures on cloth. Then, as she got older, her hands began to hurt when she sewed. So Grandma Moses decided to paint pictures instead.

4   She painted her first picture on a piece of canvas. She used house paint! At first she copied pictures from postcards. Then she began to paint things she remembered from her childhood.

5   When Grandma Moses was a young girl, she saw people using the sap from maple trees to make syrup and sugar. "Sugaring off" is a special name for this. A hole is made in the trunk of a maple tree. The tree sap drips into buckets.

Then the sap is taken to the sugar shack. There, the sap is boiled to make maple sugar. The sap is boiled in huge vats.

6   Grandma Moses painted many pictures about sugaring off. She showed people carrying buckets of sap from maple trees. She showed the boiling vats of sap and the sugar shack. To make the light on the snow dance and sparkle, Grandma Moses added touches of glitter to her painting.

7   Grandma Moses started painting when she was 75 years old. She painted over 1,600 paintings. In fact, she painted 25 pictures in the last year of her life, when she was 100 years old!

3 **Why did Grandma Moses decide to paint instead of sew? Give ONE detail from the passage to support your answer.**

_____

_____

_____

_____

_____

GO ON

Name _____ Date _____

4 **Look back at the passages "Spoonbridge and Cherry" and "Grandma Moses." Complete the Venn diagram with details from the passages.**

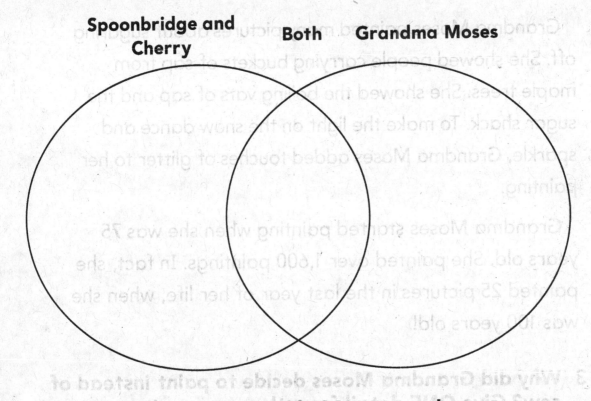

Spoonbridge and Cherry   Both   Grandma Moses

How are the passages alike? How are they different?

_____

_____

_____

_____

_____

_____

STOP

Reading/Writing Practice Test

Read the story. Then answer the questions.

Tug of War

1   A long time ago in Africa, there lived an animal named Rabbit. Rabbit liked to brag about how strong he was. "I am as strong as Elephant!" he said. "I am as strong as Hippo!"

2   Elephant and Hippo were about fifty times bigger than Rabbit, and both of them were sure that they were stronger than Rabbit. "Rabbit could never be as strong as we are," they would say when they heard Rabbit bragging.

3   Finally, Elephant got mad and challenged Rabbit to a pulling contest. "I will hold one end of a rope," he said. "You hold the other end. We'll both pull as hard as we can. We shall see who is stronger!"

4   "Give me my end of the rope," said Rabbit. "I'll go into the forest. When you hear me say 'Go!,' the contest will begin!"

5   Rabbit scampered off with the rope. He went into the woods and to the river where Hippo lived. "Hippo!" he shouted. "Let's have a pulling contest!"

GO ON ▶

6   When he saw Hippo, Rabbit held up his end of
Elephant's rope. "You take this end of the rope, while I
take the other end into the forest. When I say 'Go!,' we'll
both pull. You'll see that I'm just as strong as you!"

7   "I'll win," said Hippo confidently, and he took one end
of the rope. Rabbit ran back into the forest where no
one could see him. "Go!" he shouted.

8   Well, Hippo pulled, and Elephant pulled. They pulled as
hard as they possibly could for a whole day, but neither
of them could win the contest. And when they finally
gave up, they were exhausted.

9   Rabbit came hopping up. He didn't look tired at all! "I
guess now you'll agree that I'm just as strong as you,"
he said.

10   And they did!

**1 Why does Elephant get mad at Rabbit? Use evidence
   from the text to support your answer.**

_____

_____

_____

_____

**2 What did Rabbit do to fool Elephant and Hippo? Use
   evidence from the text to support your answer.**

_____

_____

_____

_____

_____

_____

GO ON ▶

Name _____   Date _____

Read the story. Then answer the questions.

Turtle's Trick

1   There was a big lake in Tennessee where many animals lived. One day some of the animals began boasting about what they could do.

2   "I'm the smartest of all," said Fox.

3   "Well, I'm the strongest," said Bear.

4   "No, I'm the strongest!" Turtle said.

5   Bear and Fox laughed and laughed when they heard this. When they stopped laughing, Bear said he wanted to have a pulling contest with Turtle. "We'll each take one end of a rope," he said. "Then we'll each pull as hard as we can. Do you agree?"

6   Turtle nodded. "I agree!" he said.

7   Bear and Turtle found a long rope. "You walk into the woods," Turtle said to Bear. "I'll get into the water. When I yell, pull your end of the rope just as hard as you can."

8   Bear was positive that he would win the contest. "It will be as easy as catching a fish!" he told Fox as they walked off. "I will pull for about one second, and Turtle will come flying out of the water!"

9   "You'll be the winner, Bear!" Fox said.

10   But Turtle had a tricky plan. He dived into the water with the rope, tied his end around a big tree root at the bottom of the lake, and then he swam back to the surface. "Pull!" he yelled.

11   Bear pulled with all of his might, but no matter how hard he pulled, he couldn't pull Turtle out of the lake. After a while he gave up.

12   "I guess you win," he said to Turtle the next day. "You're a lot stronger than I thought!"

13   "And smarter, too!" thought Turtle.

GO ON ▶

3 **Why do Bear and Fox laugh a lot when Turtle says he is the strongest? Use evidence from the text to support your answer.**

_____

_____

_____

_____

_____

_____

4 **Look back at "Tug of War" and "Turtle's Trick."
Complete the Venn diagram with details from
the stories.**

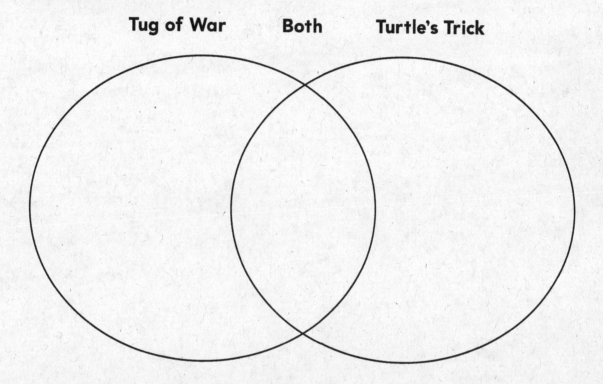

Tug of War   Both   Turtle's Trick

How are the stories alike? How are they different?

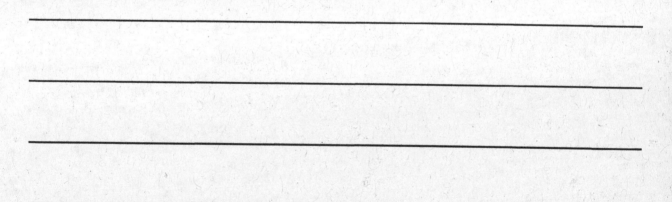

_____

_____

_____

_____

STOP

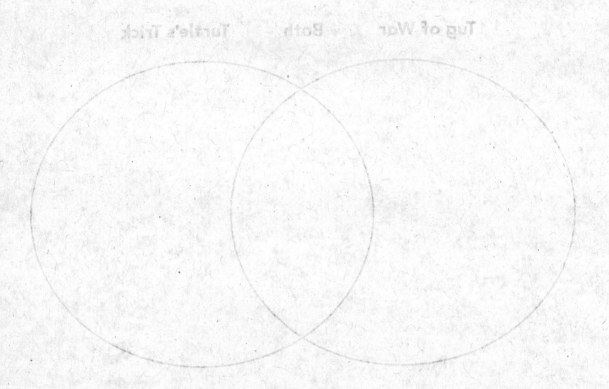